F.S.P.

F.S.P.

An N.C.O.'s Description of
His and Others' First
Six Months of War
January 1st — June 1st 1940

by

ARTHUR GWYNN-BROWNE

With two extracts from
'History and Hope'

Edited and introduced by
N.H. Reeve

seren

Seren is the book imprint of
Poetry Wales Press Ltd
Nolton Street, Bridgend, Wales
www.seren-books.com

© Arthur Gwynn-Browne, 1942
Introduction © N.H. Reeve, 2004
First published by Chatto & Windus, 1942
This edition 2004

ISBN 1-85411-373-9

A CIP record for this title is available from
the British Library.

The publisher works with the financial assistance
of the Welsh Books Council.

Cover Illustration by Lorraine Bewsey.

Printed in Plantin by CPD (Wales), Ebbw Vale.

Contents

Introduction

The year 2004 sees the centenary of a number of notable writers of the middle part of the 20th century – novelists as diverse as Graham Greene, Christopher Isherwood, Molly Keane, Patrick Hamilton, and Nancy Mitford, and poets such as Cecil Day-Lewis and Patrick Kavanagh. It is also 100 years since the birth of the almost completely forgotten Arthur Gwynn-Browne, who produced one of the most remarkable pieces of prose to appear in Britain during the Second World War: *F.S.P.*, his memoir of his service with the Field Security Personnel, attached·to the BEF during the retreat to Dunkirk. Almost as remarkable is the fact that, despite a highly-favourable initial reception, the book has now been out of print for more than 50 years. This new edition will be invaluable for the emerging critical reassessments of the literature of the 1940s, a period hitherto relatively neglected. More than this, however, the new edition will make available to today's readers an exceptionally vivid and haunting eye-witness account of one of the most traumatic events in British history, at a time when our fascination with the Second World War, and with the experiences and feelings of those who lived through it, seems more intense than ever.

F.S.P. is very different from other war memoirs. The story it tells is absorbing, affecting, thrilling, often funny; the subject matter virtually ensures this. But the extra potency lies in the arrestingly idiosyncratic manner of the telling: in the immersing of the reader from the outset in the psychological turbulence so central to that story. Gwynn-Browne's real subject is the impact upon a nearly-middle-aged civilian of the novelty, the oddity, the earnest optimism, the apprehensiveness, the raw fear, and the bitter sensation of defeat to which joining the army had brought him. The experience made him want to do fresh things with words. The novelist Elizabeth Bowen, reviewing *F.S.P.* on its publication in 1942, sensed in it 'an entirely different rhythm from all the usual rhythms of English prose'. Gwynn-Browne had 'made a break with a number of those conventions... that cling to the English language when it is written down. He writes exactly as he would speak, and punctuates (or does not punctuate) accordingly'. Bowen noted how much the experimental prose writings of Gertrude Stein had influenced 'these almost devastating simplifications, these rearrangements of rhythm to fit a feeling', and this 'mixture of truthfulness and impatience that demands short-cut innovations in written English'. But in bringing such experimentation to bear upon the tedious routines and the sudden wild upheavals of army life, Gwynn-Browne was truly a 'pioneer', his style 'adept and quite extraordinary'. 'This is skinned language,' Bowen wrote. 'Can we take it or not?'[1] Having spent four days in May 1940 on almost non-stop improvised point duty, trying to control the flood of refugees through the town of Avesnes, Gwynn-Browne's unit had moved north to Béthune, only to find more refugees being machine-gunned and bombed by German aircraft:

> What was happening was in our consciousness but our consciousness was not registering. We were living in a continuous present and anything in it was equal to anything else in it. Avesnes already seemed as if it had once hardly happened but when it had it was hard to say. Avesnes had happened yesterday. Did we feel it and know it. We could not. We were living in a continuous present and our consciousness was not registering. (p.97)

The word 'hardly', at the centre of this passage, is made to do some strenuous work. It disrupts slightly the vague, fairy-tale remoteness evoked by the word 'once' – the sentence would make less complicated sense without 'hardly', or without 'once'. It also seems to anticipate, to pre-echo 'hard', a few words later on, as if the mind under pressure were running ahead of itself, and the sentence were trying to act out, as much as to describe, the sense of temporal dislocation that bothers it. Meanwhile, the effort the passage is making towards a clear statement is distracted by the machine-gun noise in the syllable pattern, 'had-hard-hap-had-hard-had-hap'. The cultural theorist Slavoj Žižek, discussing the effects of trauma, has argued that 'we cannot ever comprehend the "whole" of reality that we encounter: if we are to be able to endure our encounter with reality, some part of it has to be "derealised", experienced as a spectral apparition'[2] – exactly as Gwynn-Browne experiences it here, using all the resources of his writing to assist him, allowing the twin meanings attached to the word 'hardly': 'with difficulty', and 'scarcely, not-quite-real', to gesture towards the heart of the traumatic, to that 'derealised' element which appears impossible to assimilate or represent in normal categories.

Later in his narrative, Gwynn-Browne will say he has 'quite clearly' remembered everything he went through; everything violent, mystifying, farcical and peculiar. 'But it was so puzzling like it had no reality. It had reality but it eluded being dealt with' (p.124). And rather than being 'dealt with', clarified or made solid, 'it' seems instead to have infiltrated the style of his writing and lodged itself there: in the twists of logic, the omissions of clinching words, the humorous and disconcerting syntactical dramatisations of the points being made – this, for example: 'And a Russian theory as everyone knows is that a Russian theory is repeatedly insoluble' (p.104) – and in the elusive, puzzling overlappings and telescopings of phrasing, so that even where the overall gist of what is being said is clear enough, new ripples of meaning seem to be emerging before the first ones have quite settled. Sheltering as best he could from the German bombers, in a little copse just outside Dunkirk where 'time seemed suspended', he said to himself:

> I will not be killed, I will not be killed I have things to do I will not be killed like this I will not be killed like this I have things to do like this I will not be killed like this. And then I felt yes all the indignation and yes all the humiliation of it that there we were lying like animals there in a wood here and there they were dropping things on us up there to kill us like animals were down here. (p.125)

There is nothing quite comparable to this in the other literature of the time. As Elizabeth Bowen pointed out in her review, most writers of the war, certainly in its earlier stages, were more concerned with producing unvarnished records than with 'innovations in the shaping of sentences'. Partly because there did not seem to be enough time available for imaginative exploring, but also because wartime experiences themselves appeared, in the opinion of many, to be setting intractable difficulties for the artist approaching them. Bowen argued elsewhere that 'these years rebuff the imagination as much by being fragmentary as by being violent'; the writer's quest for order and meaning was interrupted by too many 'recurrent checks'.[3] For William Sansom, 'the dreadful performance of modern battle' was 'too violent for the arts to transcribe'; the arts would for the time being have to content themselves with more modest objectives, sketching the passing fragments with a view to establishing a coherence later, once normal conditions for meaning had recurred.[4] Stephen Spender felt that much of the artistic experimentation still being conducted had in any case been rendered virtually redundant by events; the subversive distortions and dream landscapes of Surrealism, for example, were becoming over-familiar and losing their weird potency: 'Its "objects" hurtle around our heads, its operations cause the strangest conjunctions of phenomena in the most unexpected places, its pronouncements fill the newspapers'.[5] But for Gwynn-Browne, the war seems not to have inhibited creativity but to have released it. He shared the contemporary desire to keep a diary of one's impressions, to assemble a kind of emotional archive to be drawn upon in future tranquillity. But where he differs is in his willingness to allow the problematic elements, the 'checks' in the experience, to register straight away, at the level of writing itself, producing what Bowen called those 'painful', 'cryptic' sentences which 'throb like exposed nerves', and take us so disturbingly close to the moment: 'The effect, as one reads, is that everything ... is happening to oneself'.[6]

Gwynn-Browne had undergone no apprenticeship as a writer. He had published nothing before *F.S.P.* He was born William Arthur Browne, on December 13, 1904, not far from the Welsh border; the son of a Shrewsbury corn merchant, whose own father had been Mayor of the town. He was educated at

Malvern and subsequently at Christ Church, Oxford, which he left in 1927; illness appears to have prevented him from taking a degree, although he was master of the Christ Church Beagles. W.H. Auden, a few years younger, was also at Christ Church, as was the aesthete Harold Acton, but it is not clear whether Gwynn-Browne became acquainted with either. By the time he went up to Oxford he was signing himself 'W.A.G. Browne', and shortly afterwards he decided to complete the Welsh-sounding conversion of his surname. Judging from some surviving correspondence, his two sisters also appear to have done so, although his mother, who lived with him in his last years, continued to be known as 'Mrs Browne'. Rather bewilderingly, his father's name was Arthur Browne, his paternal grandfather's name was William Browne, and his mother's father's name was originally Arthur William Brown, so the young William Arthur may have had any number of reasons for desiring an alteration. It was not uncommon, however, for such name-changes to be made for inheritance purposes – his maternal grandfather had become Arthur William Sparrow for just that reason – and this change may have had something to do with the collapse, in 1927, of Gwynn-Browne's father's business, owing to a cargo loss at sea, which forced the family to leave their fairly imposing, albeit rented residence, Hanwood House, near Shrewsbury. At any rate, Arthur began his working life very modestly, as a stores-and-cellarman in a small Cardiff hotel; he subsequently became a receptionist in London, and eventually manager of the Sheringham Hotel, Sheringham, in Norfolk, before joining up in December 1939, around the time of his 35th birthday. What happened to him over the following six months forms the subject of his book.

Although there is no record of his having had literary ambitions prior to this, he had certainly developed a keen interest in the work of the American modernist Gertrude Stein. His description of himself at Béthune, 'living in a continuous present', marks one of his many adaptations of Stein's ideas and methods to his own needs. She first used the phrase 'continuous present' in a lecture entitled 'Composition as Explanation', which Gwynn-Browne may well have heard when she delivered it in Oxford in 1926, and which Leonard and Virginia Woolf published at their Hogarth Press later the same year.[7] Stein was attempting, without stepping outside her style in order to analyse it, to describe how her writing was always in search of re-creation in each moment, constantly untying itself from its past. She would use slightly-varying repetitions, for example, or would detach words from their usual connotations, taking away the reference-points around which narrative order and succession would normally be organised. In prose passages such as the *Portraits*, she had experimented with a kind of linguistic Cubism, constructing an image from a jostle of numerous simultaneous, interpenetrating materials and perspectives; and when Gwynn-Browne writes of his 'continuous present' that 'anything in it was equal to anything else in it', it is as if he were suddenly experiencing the world as a Cubist painting, which no single vantage-point could command, and where the relative significance or density of the component particles could no longer be readily distinguished. In 1946 Stein would say, almost in uncanny echo of her British admirer, that 'in composition one thing is as important as another thing'.[8] She had commented in 'Composition as Explanation' on how living through the tumultuous shock of the First World War had enabled her contemporaries at last to appreciate her kind of modernism; it was only then, when the nineteenth-century model of experience clearly no longer held good, that 'everyone became consciously became aware of the existence of the authenticity of the modern composition'.[9] Now, for Gwynn-Browne, a new war seemed to be bringing modernism alive again, not dulling its impact as Stephen Spender had implied; the Steinian method, or a derivation from it, was the perfect medium for current conditions:

> The continuous present ... allows the most astonishing emphasis to be given when it is necessary even when at times it may not seem necessary ... In living the most astonishing emphasis is happening in a few seconds and nothing for some days is happening makes warfare what warfare is like is the continuous present.

This passage, the only account Gwynn-Browne gives of why he chose to write as he did, is not from *F.S.P.* but from the two-part 'Diary' section of an unfinished 'Work In Progress' which he intended to call 'History and Hope': the extract is dated 18 December 1941 (p.145 below). This 'Diary', which includes an enthralling evocation of the Blitz in London, together with some intriguing meditations on the nature of Britishness, is the only other piece he is known to have written using his Steinian method, and it is published here for the first time, as an appendix to *F.S.P.*

That method is not, however, only suited to the spectacular moments of drama and chaos. It can also help to convey the sense in which joining the army was rather like becoming a child again, entering a condition which truly seemed a 'continuous present', shorn of history, on which neither memory nor expectation could reliably bear:

> One of the things about army life is how seldom what is going to happen does happen and when it does it happens differently. In peace as in war anything can happen but in war it happens much less often because the variety is so much less that what can happen is restricted to a choice. It is a choice and who chooses and why in choosing one why not choose both and why in choosing both why not choose one. Naturally not the same one. So anything that happens first does not and later if it does it happens differently.
>
> (p.3)

The satirical presentation of army absurdity resembles that in Henry Reed's famous poem 'Naming of Parts'; but there is another tone in this passage as well, the tone of someone intrigued and even a little startled by the idea that genuinely fresh possibilities of response might actually be latent in the absurdity, and beginning to push their way out of it. At 35, with a decade of working life behind him, Gwynn-Browne would have been considerably older than most of those being subjected to the adjustment of outlook, the overhaul of identity which joining up entailed; what for his comrades would have been their initiation into adulthood would for him have been closer to a mid-life reconstruction. His account of drilling gives a flavour of this:

About drilling there is not much to say.
As everybody knows it has it and does it why also say it, what it is it
is. It looks it as it is and doing it is all it looks it is but more so. How
much more so.   (p.10)

(This sounds, incidentally, like a distant recall of another line
from 'Composition as Explanation', where Stein talked of how a
composition was formed from the unique vision of each generation: 'it confuses, it shows, it is, it looks, it likes it as it is, and this
makes what is seen as it is seen'.)[10] There are vibrations in
Gwynn-Browne's sentences as of a new existence struggling into
being: subject and object seem to blur together, not yet fully
distinct, and a little tremor of fluidity is injected by the participle
'doing' into the insistent, fivefold repetition of 'it is'. There is a
rhythm of the clipped, barked parade-ground instructions; and
at the same time a rhythm of words dancing, gliding, almost
gambolling in a sheltered field, where units of meaning as well as
soldiers' feet can shift to and fro, or reverse direction, or try
something over a slightly different way. It adds to the sense
conveyed elsewhere in the book of the army as a kind of maternal body, patiently providing for all possible needs – one's idea
of what constitutes 'need' having first been stripped down and
reassembled:

So we counted out our clothing. This was the first thing the army
did do for us and I do remember so well being so impressed what
the army could do and did do this thing for each one of us. What
was impressive was that what there was of it was everything we had
we needed no more and no less. This was interesting to know ... the
army's answer to every one that it really is efficient when it does
matter and its men yes they do matter and each one of its men yes
he does matter.   (p.9)

Here, Gwynn-Browne's hotel-manager's eye is dilated with
boyish wonder. Later, on board ship for France:

Someone still had time to think of all those thousands of paper bags
of food for the troops ... at the right time in the right place in the
right numbers. Most people do find it a fearful nuisance to pack up

> a picnic lunch for six. But up to sixty and six hundred what the
> British army does for its men does not let them be a fearful nuisance
> up to six thousand and six and sixty thousand. I think this thought-
> ful touch did give us all a feeling of assurance that come what might
> we would not be forgotten. (p.28)

By way of what Elizabeth Bowen called Gwynn-Browne's
'breathless and ruthless naivety' one can feel all his frightened
excitement, his clinging for security, the pathos behind the thrill
of big numbers; and the way in which, following Stein's example,
words and phrases seem to take on fractionally different inflec-
tions each time they recur, easing in and out of alignment with
their connotations of a moment ago, so that whatever happens
next 'happens differently'.

It is this off-to-war mixture of jauntiness and anxiety, something virtually all his comrades must have shared, which *F.S.P.*
so memorably captures. Sometimes one element prevails, sometimes the other; sometimes the two seem hard to disentangle:

> Identity is one of the things it really is impossible to argue about, if
> you are you then your papers can not make you more you and if you
> are not you and your papers say you are you then how can you be
> you if you are not you, and that is identity. (p.59)

At one moment this sounds like a precursor of the *Goon
Show*. At the next, it sounds almost at the end of its tether, an
exasperated cry for simplification beyond reach of dissent. And
both these elements inadvertently draw attention to some of the
real emotional and psychological difficulties of wartime life –
with duality, with the unconscious, with not being sure whether
the breach in the continuity of the self, the second childhood,
represents a loss or an emancipation: 'how can you be you if you
are not you'? These are difficulties, moreover, which the passage
does not currently want to address, skating over them instead
with what can seem a rather ominous unconcern. And as the
story gathers pace, the writing increasingly often suggests a
psyche under threat, trying to hold itself together with rapid,
brittle formulations that offer just enough control over an experience to help one get past it: at an extreme, like this –

You could think clearly inside you but not outside you. It was shock
ofcourse (*sic*). Later on you could think outside you but nothing
responded from inside you, and that was tiredness. We walked on.

(p.126)

The pattern of inversion and repetition, and the facile fluency
it creates, seems to indicate the presence of a further symptom
underneath the symptoms that are actually described: the desire
to fence something in quickly and leave it behind before the
fencing starts to unravel.

Gwynn-Browne writes about mental disturbance at some
length, as well as half-consciously revealing it in action. Sizeable
portions of both *F.S.P.* and the 'Diary' are given over to considering whether entire populations, French and British, might be
on the point of a collective nervous breakdown, and how they
might respond to what may be about to overwhelm them. He
draws on Gertrude Stein's observations of the French national
character – showing how he took her opinions seriously, and had
an interest in her work extending beyond matters of technique –
and, in the 'Diary', on Anna Freud's psychoanalytical commen-
tary on the British reaction to the Blitz. In his 1945 novel *Gone
For A Burton*, too, he was as concerned as any British war-writer
with questions of shock, hysteria, and the mind's immune
system, its capacity to rebalance itself. Even though *F.S.P.* was
written early in 1941, after the immediate danger of a cross-
Channel invasion had passed, it is remarkable how vividly the
book is able to convey, both directly and between its lines, the
atmosphere of deep foreboding in the early summer of 1940,
when it seemed almost certain that Britain as well as France
would shortly be overrun and occupied; when no-one could be
sure, beneath the propagandist rhetoric, exactly how the people
would react; and when the Dunkirk evacuees like himself, resting
in camps in southern England, were ordered by their officers not
to talk about what they had seen: 'Think of the peace these
people enjoy and let them yes let them retain it unspoiled for the
few short weeks they may have to enjoy it. Do not spoil it while
it lasts' (p.137).

Serving in the Field Security Personnel could have given Gwynn-Browne a peculiar insight into these questions, since he and his colleagues were deployed in a forlorn attempt to forestall precisely the outbreaks of panic that most preoccupied him. At the same time, the rapidity of the retreat to Dunkirk meant that each successive 'field' had to be abandoned in dismay just as they were attempting to secure it. The F.S.P. was a non-combatant counter-sabotage unit, made up of fluent French speakers, whose rôle was to mingle with civilians, assess morale, collect information on activities potentially helpful to the enemy, and test the security of their own army's installations. The undercover nature of much of their work meant they could never really mix with the regular troops, and were often in danger of being lumped together with the hated military police – as on one occasion early on, when Gwynn-Browne was wrongly accused of having informed on some soldiers involved in a drunken brawl in a café. It was during this incident that his eye had 'caught the outline of a shape in the room's dark corner':

> Through the haze of our smoking I saw a large double bed dirty and crumpled and on it sitting up and staring in a fixed and frightened way two small children, a little boy and girl clasping each other, mute and petrified with fear. The woman with the bottles called out an oath to them and with a stifled cry they shrank and burrowed under the bed clothes and lay there stretched and shivering, more terrified of what they could not see but only feel and hear as the night wore on ... I said we must be going and we went from that place. (p.42)

There seems here to be a larger sense of inarticulate terror than the one actually described – something lying in the corner of consciousness, dimly emerging from the haze and shadow which had hidden it: terror not just as to what may be happening out of sight, but that the bond of child and mother, on which one's sense of reassurance depended, might at any moment break down, and reveal the mother to be the intensifier rather than the soother of one's fears. And in the face of so charged an image of everything that must be prevented from taking the mind over, Gwynn-Browne's Steinian prose suddenly and strikingly gives way to something more like the straight reportage that other writers used – as if in an effort to defuse the danger by putting a frame around the scene, hedging it with carefully-observed detail, and holding it off for inspection. Perhaps his army training drills played a part in this manoeuvre; automatised reactions could begin to blank out the dishevelled human ones. But by the time he reached Dunkirk, his unit having dispersed into frightened and exhausted groups with no-one left to command them, neither this kind of wary professional detachment nor his earlier bluff nonchalance could stave the impact off; we come instead upon a completely 'skinned language', an extraordinary maimed lyricism of the mind clinging with its last strength to what little is left to it:

> I lay on the wet sand and everything was surges of it ... There was a yellow noise kept coming at a very great speed to a very great distance. I could not think I could only repeat what I tried to think if I could if only a ship. If I could only if only a ship if I could and if only a ship. If I could only if only a ship if I could only one foot on a ship. If only one foot on a ship if I could only if only a ship.
>
> (p.133)

It would be hard to imagine a more powerful realisation of the 'continuous present' as an unremitting torment, in which the disrupted repetitions are this time both yearning for finality and warding it off.

The closing pages of the book, with their accumulation of part-echoes, revisitings and permutations of phrasing, suggest an infinitesimally gradual disengagement from the repercussions of that 'yellow noise' which nonetheless persist. And once he is safely back in England, seeing the foodstalls set up for the evacuees on stations by women volunteers, his disconnected feeling attaches itself to a euphoric, homecoming vision of the feminine, reclaimed now as the true source of reassurance:

> In their cotton frocks and smiling and just as they had been yesterday that made today like yesterday and today like any day. We did not know what was today but they did make today today ... They had clean bright cotton frocks and neat hair and silk stockings they

were cheerful and smiling and they were not ... it was so important
to us that they were not refugees. They had been like yesterday what
they were today and that made them not refugees and we were not
and then at last we were not any different ... the buttercups were
sheets of gold in meadow after meadow and oxeye daisies spangled
them and cow parsley like a bride's veil drifting.   (pp.136-7)

Are not passages like these, poignant enough already, made
the more so by the profound sense of survivor guilt that seems
to underpin them?

The publication of *F.S.P.* was delayed for the best part of a year
by the War Office. No serving soldier's memoir of Dunkirk was
allowed to appear in print before the official Despatches of Lord
Gort, the commander of the B.E.F., were published, early in
1942. The War Office also objected to several passages in *F.S.P.*
as being potentially prejudicial to morale; in particular, they
ordered the publishers to remove a reference to French officers
commandeering cars, loading them with their own families and
possessions, and driving away from the front. Given the rapidity
with which the débâcle of Dunkirk had been mythologised into a
British triumph, there was acute sensitivity to Gwynn-Browne's
having touched on the kinds of suppressed reaction which would
be detailed at length in Ian McEwan's novel *Atonement*, for
example: the anger felt on the beaches at the apparent absence of
the RAF, and at the self-serving behaviour of some of the officers
in charge. Letters written late in 1941 show how anxious
Gwynn-Browne was not to be thought to have implied that the
officers had left their men in the lurch; he told his publisher,
Harold Raymond of Chatto and Windus, to impress upon the
War Office that 'the absence of officers was the temporary delu-
sion of a bewildered mind'. But by now it appears that apart from
his desire to get his book past the censors, Gwynn-Browne had
other reasons for wishing to placate officialdom; he was trying to
engineer a transfer into the RAF and out of the Army Catering
Corps, into which, much to his chagrin, he had been seconded
some time after the evacuation (presumably on account of his
background in hotel management).

The humiliating secondment had at least provided him with some time to write. He produced a short story, 'What Beasts Men Are', based on his pre-war hotel experiences and entirely conventional in style; it appeared in the December 1942 issue of *Penguin New Writing*. He pressed on with drafts and scraps of 'History and Hope', an ambitious semi-philosophical rhapsody in which he called for a highly-personalised form of socialist revolution; and in 1942-3 he wrote his only novel, *Gone For A Burton*. This is a tale of four RAF aircrew, shot down over occupied France and eventually escaping. It very effectively conveys the extreme youth of the airmen, their utter ignorance of anything foreign, their resentful arrogance towards anyone outside their special orbit; it shows how bomber crews could inhabit a virtual reality in which the actual consequences of the bombs they dropped scarcely registered with them; it emphasises, again, the mothering element in service life, how completely dependent these boys were on their cocoons of cockpit, barracks, and RAF in-jokes and behaviour codes. The latent tensions between the crew members, and the hysterical outbursts resulting from their sudden exposure to reality, are well detailed, as is the cavalier and almost idiotic insouciance that helps keep them going. The novel does in its way secrete its author's deeply mixed feelings about Forces life, and his fantasy of a future in which the supreme efficiency and competence of the RAF as an organisation could in some way be integrated with a wider human sensitivity; also, the homoerotic element latent in *F.S.P.* seems more marked here, without of course ever being brought fully into the open.

Gone For A Burton is well worth reading, but, as with 'What Beasts Men Are', the actual writing is disappointingly conventional. Gwynn-Browne had been persuaded by his publisher to abandon the Steinian influence and attempt something more approachable. Harold Raymond was clearly troubled by the rejection of *F.S.P.* by Random House in New York, on the grounds that 'its point of view and its humor are so British that ... it would not, in our view, appeal to American readers'[11] – so much for Gertrude Stein – and when writing to American publishers on Gwynn-Browne's behalf Raymond assured them that the coming work would have nothing outlandish in it. (There had in fact already been something faintly apologetic about the way Chatto and Windus had promoted *F.S.P.* themselves; the dust-jacket blurb talked of the comedy and the thought-provoking element in the book while saying virtually nothing about the style.) But the end-result of these negotiations, *Gone For A Burton*, was a fairly straightforward, intermittently interesting escape story, weighed down by weak characterisation and unconvincing dialogue; doing its best to be stirring and exciting, but unable really to reproduce any of the immediacy and rawness of *F.S.P.*, or the sense of that elusive, puzzling 'it', the hallucinatory terror of warfare, the un-nameable convulsion which had sent its ripples through Gwynn-Browne's earlier book from the first page to the last.

Gone For A Burton was the last work he completed. He abandoned 'History and Hope' after numerous false starts, and nothing else appears to have gone beyond the note-making stage. The war seems to have scarred him, physically and mentally, in ways from which he perhaps never quite recovered; it seems to have both given him his writing and taken it away. He saw no further active service. In the summer of 1943 he was the subject of an army psychiatrist's report which stressed the importance of his being interviewed by someone in civilian clothes, as the mere sight of a uniform seemed to provoke a hostile reaction. In December 1944 he was appointed Home Bursar of Magdalen College, Oxford, where he stayed for some years, planning a novel about hotel life and sketching a symphony, without finishing either. In September 1950 he resigned his post, after what he described as 'a prolonged and gruelling breakdown in health';[12] two years later, the last unsold copies of *F.S.P.* were pulped. Gwynn-Browne went to live for a time in London, before finally moving, in 1961, to an old vicarage in Mere, Wiltshire, where he spent his last years as a virtual recluse, with his elderly mother and a manservant to look after them. None of his neighbours, who knew him as 'Archie', had the least idea that he had ever been a writer. He died in October 1964, aged 59.

The text of *F.S.P.* is taken from the 1942 edition. Gwynn-Browne's idiosyncratic spellings and usages (e.g. 'ofcourse', 'noone') have been preserved. The two extracts from 'History and Hope' are taken from Gwynn-Browne's own working typescripts, the only form in which the work appears to survive. These typescripts are not in a finished state; they contain some minor hand-revisions, and notes in the margin at points where the author felt further revision would be necessary (e.g. the paragraph beginning 'Yet even so', on p.157).

NOTES

1. Elizabeth Bowen, 'With Silent Friends', *The Tatler and Bystander*, 5 August, 1942, p.182.
2. Slavov Žižek, *The Fright of Real Tears*, London: BFI Publishing, 2001, p.68.
3. Elizabeth Bowen, 'Contemporary', *The New Statesman*, 23 May 1942; also quoted in Robert Hewison, *Under Siege: Literary Life in London 1939-45*, London: Weidenfeld and Nicolson, 1977, p.88. Further comments on contemporary attitudes towards wartime writing can be found in *Under Siege*, especially pp.87-90, and in Rod Mengham's essay 'Broken Glass', in *The Fiction of the 1940s: Stories of Survival*, eds. R. Mengham and N.H. Reeve, Basingstoke and New York: Palgrave, 2001, p.125. Hewison makes a passing reference to *F.S.P.* on his page 90, but only as one in a list of 'Army novels' (*sic*). Mengham briefly discusses Gwynn-Browne's political views in *The Idiom of the Time: The Writings of Henry Green*, Cambridge: Cambridge University Press, 1982, pp.57-8.
4. William Sansom, 'A Fireman's Journal', in *Leaves in the Storm: A Book of Diaries*, eds. Stefan Schimanski and Henry Treece, London: Lindsay Drummond, 1947, p.141.
5. Stephen Spender, 'Some Observations on English Poetry between Two Wars', in *Transformation*, no. 3, eds. Stefan Schimanski and Henry Treece, London: Lindsay Drummond, 1945, p.3.
6. Elizabeth Bowen, 'With Silent Friends', p.184.
7. Gertrude Stein, 'Composition as Explanation', in *Selected Writings of Gertrude Stein*, ed. Carl Van Vechten, New York: Vintage Books, 1990, p.518.
8. 'A Transatlantic Interview – 1946', in *A Primer for the Gradual Understanding of Gertrude Stein*, ed. Robert Bartlett Haas, Los Angeles: Black Sparrow Press, 1973, p.15.
9. 'Composition as Explanation', p.521.
10. 'Composition as Explanation', p.516.
11. Letter from Random House Inc to Harold Raymond of Chatto and Windus Ltd, of 27 January 1943, in the archives of the University of Reading.
12. Letter from Arthur Gwynn-Browne to Harold Raymond, 15 February 1951, in the archives of the University of Reading.

N.H. Reeve

To
Lieut. C.J.F. Ashby
C.S.M. Laversuch
&
The members of
No. 30 Section, F.S.P.
serving under them

Foreword

I AM in the F.S.P.

F.S.P. stands for Field Security Personnel.

That is the authorized version.

There are conflicting interpretations in the vulgate which though picturesque are misleading.

When Tim Ashby our first officer wrote and said he had never heard the story of our escape from France because by then he was ill in hospital I wrote and told him. He wrote back and said it was rather awful my story had come when they were on manoeuvres, it had been passed round, the manoeuvres had stopped, and the B.G.S. then read it through from cover to over. What a B.G.S. is in the authorized version I do not know but in the vulgate—well anyway he read it.

Tim Ashby then said if that is the story of your escape from France why not do it from the beginning before you got to France. So I did and have done it.

I ought to say just one more thing before I begin. F.S.P. are scheduled as non-combatant troops. That is why there is nothing heroic in this account of what we did in France and in our training for it. We did nothing heroic at all. The fighting and the heroism were done all round us by the combatant troops but we the non-combatant troops looked on and were saved. I think there are about seven times more non-combatant troops than combatant ones in the British army and in any army and we are some of them.

About the names of people. Anyone trying to recognize himself and doing so will be put through Part II Orders and prosecuted. Except Section Thirty. Anyone in Section Thirty knows too much about anyone else in it to need prosecuting.

Well anyway read on.

A. G-B.

Inverness

April 1941

PART ONE: THE BEGINNING

1. Starting

EVERYTHING had been arranged and Monday followed Sunday. We were about sixty of us and on motor bicycles on the barrack square.

We looked very smart and able one by one and in leaving the barracks if anyone broke down there was a car behind to do whatever could be done. Everything was polished and gleaming and though very heavy it still was a pleasure to be leaving and well yes we were leaving at last and for good. We thought so.

Everything had been arranged to take place and then everything was rearranged not to take place and then it was Monday, then it was arranged we should go we did not go and then we did go on that Monday. Or was it Sunday.

One of the things about army life is how seldom what is going to happen does happen and when it does it happens differently. In peace as in war anything can happen but in war it happens much less often because the variety is so much less that what can happen is restricted to a choice. It is a choice and who chooses and why in choosing one why not choose both and why in choosing both why not choose one. Naturally not the same one. So anything that happens first does not and later if it does it happens differently.

In army life it is simple. Monday follows Sunday and if anything does happen when it does then well why not.

Well anyway we started.

We were bound for Southampton.

Soon after leaving and being outside the area of jurisdiction over which our commanders had sufficient influence to be obeyed we were stopped and they counted us. Counting takes time. The man who was chosen as a good one for counting went up and

3

down the line of us counting and when he got up to sixty he went down the line the other way counting. Then when he got up to sixty again he knew the first time of counting had been right and he said so and we were all very pleased and relieved. They said yes sixty agrees with the documents we have signed and you say there are sixty men and that is all right so far as it goes but we have also sixty motor bicycles that is very important and where are they. Well anyway the problem was solved by agreeing that who ever had got to where we were had done it by motor bicycling and if sixty had done it it was surprising but not unbelievable. Counting is not unbelievable if you do it often enough and that is the reason for counting.

We started up our engines but before going on they said stop them. It was worrying. A few weeks ago another lot of us had left the barracks and everyone had said goodbye and it was very exciting like it was the end of term. Then in the evening they had all come back again. It was not a mistake it was like what I said, what had happened to them had been restricted to a choice and the later choice had not been like the first choice and that was all. This lot now was with us and well it was worrying for them. Saying twice goodbye is difficult but three times saying it is cynical.

What they said was take off all our ornaments. We then knew then there was no more going back. We were outside the area of the jurisdiction of our commanders and taking off our ornaments put us beyond their range of recognition. We removed our arm bands cap badges shoulder titles and every thing the barracks was so proud of that distinguished us as what we were. When we looked like what the barracks would not have recognized or if they had recognized would have put us on a dozen charges for not conforming to the regulations of being improperly dressed we started up our engines and we went on and we did not once look back.

The army was on location, we knew it, and were we glad.

Southampton is a long way well it is in convoy. Just outside it we were stopped by soldiers in the road who stuck on labels on our headlights for the purposes of embarkation. Some women appeared from a house and provided us with cups of tea and pieces of cake. We had had breakfast at half past seven it was now half past two so you can imagine and they would not take a penny. It really is such acts of kindness make you wonder whether you do do enough. They would not take a penny.

We drove down to the docks, put our machines in a big shed and emptied them of petrol. They put a rubber tube in to the tank and we pumped it out in to a barrel then what was left over we ran the engines on until there was no more not one drop. This all took time it was four oclock and then some buses came and we got into them.

We were driven outside Southampton that is there were trees not houses and then up a drive and more trees and then a small house in the middle of them. We got out. They said this is a camp and seven of you go in there. I went in it was a study that is it was one once and now we were more than seven we were eleven. I went in like everyone else I always choose a corner and I did so, and when we had put everything we had on our backs in heaps on the floor they gave us two blankets and there we were to sleep there.

I do not remember washing but we went into a tent on a lawn and we had our meal it was a hot one it was not very nice but we did still feel better after having had it.

I think then we were free to do what we liked, anyway everyone went. I went into the garden it was evening and quite warm it was a big garden with flowering shrubs lawns shady paths and concealed quiet places. I sat down under a tree.

Everyone had gone, it was very still and peaceful. I was alone.

It was the first day of April and this I am writing this the first day of April but then everything was to come. A whole year of it was to come and indeed it has come the first day of April now and then it was the first day of April I was alone at last for the first time alone, at last I was alone. I had not been alone no not really since I had joined up when I had was in December nineteen thirty-nine, what a long time ago that seemed. Today that is one year ago today was the first day of April nineteen hundred and forty and could I remember before that and could I begin thinking.

It was still and peaceful sitting still under the tree and I began thinking.

It was the evening of our first day. We had started on our task.

2 Training

We were three or four days more in the rest camp and there were more than sixty of us many more and more kept coming. Who ran the rest camp I think it was the RASC and how kind they were. We were more than they could really accommodate but everything they could do they did for us and there was no shouting ordering and fussing. After being in the barracks it was like being out again amongst grown up people. It was very strange and satisfying.

We had not much to do. We went down to the docks and loaded things on ships and we had a bath and Southampton was very nice it was clean looking with big wide streets wide enough for the trams not to be a trouble, and there were trees and houses in big gardens with them. Of course all this now is in ruins but it is nice to know that Southampton was nice enough before they make it better.

We had times to keep and we had to be in for meals but between them we did do what we wanted to do and it was just like being grown up. It really was assumed we would not inevitably be negligent disobedient stupid and perverse and that after what we had been assumed to be inevitably was really strange and satisfying.

I mostly walked in the garden or sat in it and reviewed what had been happening until it gradually became clearer and gradually yes it did. What happens to anyone who joins up is approximately the same as to anyone else whether it gradually becomes clearer to them or never is clear at all. Still it always is nice to know what has happened to you at least I think so.

Why I joined up was like everybody else I had a confused feeling I wanted to do something and the easiest thing was to do it. Then too I did want to stop feeling civilized and to know what discomfort could do to you. I always have been comfortable that is I always have had what I wanted to have it has not been much, I have not been very materially ambitious, but never mind I have had it. Most people have had it oh yes they have had it because they always look back to the times of peace as being desirable and that is comfortable and each one has been comfortable in his comfortable way. Not everyone but has warfare made these less comfortable ones more comfortable not at all, they all have been comfortable most people have all been quite comfortable whatever it is that they say.

I must say immediately on joining up I knew what discomfort was so did we all but knowing what it feels like is not the same thing as knowing what it does to you. That comes later. What it does to you is nothing, discomfort does nothing to you. That is one of the real discoveries about living differently and joining up that everyone makes that comfort and discomfort are comparative terms and anything is more comfortable than it might be. It might be worse. When the first day we got to our barracks we were about thirty of us in a wooden hut, it was freezing so hard it had to be kept secret, you remember how freezing that whole winter was and it could not be published till afterwards, they gave us two blankets and they said there you are. Well yes there we were. There was no fire, the light had been stolen, the boards were bare, and where we had walked and stood it was melting snow. We undressed we lay down. That was discomfort and could it be worse. Well I have always thought in moments of stress of the Poles and Jews the Germans put in locked up trains until they froze to death, and then later on I have thought of people bombed out of their homes, shocked destitute and overwhelmed, so what was my discomfort to theirs. Could it be worse yes much. Anything can be worse and physical discomfort can always be much worse.

Once you stop being civilized and having everything you want your body comes to the rescue and it seldom lets you down. It really is astonishing what the human body can endure and I am glad I know it. I do think everybody should be glad to know it.

What the mind can endure is quite a different thing than what the body can but now I am just saying what the human body can endure is astonishing how it does just come to the rescue.

After discovering discomfort and how little it matters I next discovered the army and how efficient it is. This was much more surprising than discomfort because everyone had expected discomfort but who had expected efficiency. Well I had not and I was impressed and I continually am being impressed that the army really is efficient and really is immensely efficient, not always no it is not always but when it is it is immensely efficient. Ofcourse it has to be and that makes it more interesting and more impressive than if it need not be. Any one can be efficient if it does not matter but can they be efficient if it does matter. I think that is really the army's answer to every one, it really is efficient when it does matter.

On the third day after beginning we were all lined up and we went into a big room where we were to be clothed. We were a good many of us and there was a good deal to be given to us and to each one of us and then we went out and then we were done each one.

It did not take long. We took with us every thing we had to the wooden huts where we now were sleeping and laid our clothing on our beds. I shall not soon forget the pleasure I had in my great coat and the hope that at last I might possibly be warm. The cold was so intense, we were in a piercing wind on a hill there was nothing to do and we had been inoculated, no fires were allowed before six in the evening, later on when they got a new medical officer the first thing he did was to have all the fires lit in the morning, but then I was in hospital so my pleasure was posthumous. Still the others all did have it to enjoy it did revive them.

Well anyway we counted out our clothing on our beds. These beds were not like civilian beds in fact they were called biscuits but the principle was the same you lay down on them with the intention of sleeping. There are three biscuits like large dog biscuits the same colour and shape and you have three blankets and by arrangement you can have three thicknesses below you and three thicknesses above you. By degrees you do not worry so much about what is below you and then finally you do not worry about anything below you. I have slept on practically anything below me. However biscuits were the first of everything to come and the principle is the same, you lie down on what is below you with the intention of sleeping. The intention to begin with is what is most restful.

So we counted out our clothing. This was the first thing the army did do for us and I do remember so well being so impressed what the army could do and did do this thing for each one of us. What was impressive was that what there was of it was everything we had we needed no more and no less. This was interesting to know. In civilian living you do most generally have too much of one thing and too little of another so what you really do need you never do know. In packing for instance what do you know if you are civilized you do not know and if you are considerably civilized you then have to hire some other one to do your packing for you because really being civilized you do not know.

Anyway I knew just what I needed no more and no less, and since that day I have never needed any other thing. Yes just one thing pyjamas and a mirror they are not necessary, I just do want them but I do not need them.

Looking at my things I thought if I was a poor man without one penny I would still be well and warmly clad and would have the means of keeping myself clean and proper without spending one more penny. Every thing of its kind was good and useful adequate and sensible and I did not need to spend one penny.

Later on when I saw the French and Belgian armies I remembered this about the British army what the British army does do first for its men. That is the army's answer to every one that it really is efficient when it does matter and its men yes they do matter and each one of its men yes he does matter.

After dressing we began drilling.

About drilling there is not much to say.

As everybody knows it has it and does it why also say it, what it is it is. It looks it as it is and doing it is all it looks it is but more so. How much more so.

Drilling is difficult because it involves discipline leadership and character and what they are. What is difficult is the connection between what they are and what any of them are in their connection with each other is what is so difficult. How much does each of them need of the other for instance leadership and character need less drilling and discipline and too much of one affects the other. It is very difficult. What is more difficult is when drilling and discipline have less of leadership and character than is necessary for them to maintain themselves. They become then just shouting and rage repression punishments and suppressed confusion and inevitably what happens is they have to become more so to maintain themselves at all. That is what happened to us, it was interesting but it was difficult and was it important. Well yes it was important not so much for us as for them who were making it. Well what happened happened and with what results.

What drilling really is is instruction in the simplest way of doing anything with ability and ease.

Discipline is the next stage, it reinforces what the response is to what is ordered to be done and its purpose is to ensure that the greatest number respond and do it with the least complication.

Without drilling first and discipline afterwards several thousand different men could never do a single thing together with ability and ease and have precision in so doing. They could not even if they wanted to and anything you want to do is easier than doing it if you have to, so drilling and discipline are both necessary and helpful. They should be. But drilling and discipline would not be sufficient to achieve their purpose unless the thing to be done was the simplest way of doing it and it always interested me to see what trouble had been taken in making a simple action as simple as possible. A great deal of trouble had been taken and it was worth while taking a great deal of trouble to do whatever they wanted you to do in the way they wanted you to do it.

Anything simple to do is difficult to do because it is a simplification of several much more probable ways of doing it. Turning round for instance anyone can turn round when they please and as often as they please but can they turn round as easily as when they are told when to do it. Not at all. And can they turn round too when some one else does turn round too and are they then together not necessarily not necessarily at all because each one has his own more probable way of doing it than the other one and that is what happens. They do not turn round they get round. Anyway we turned round and when we had mastered the difficulty of the simplest way of doing it we then turned round together.

There is a reason for everything if it is explained. To begin with it was explained, we had a sergeant a very good sergeant he explained what we had to do and how to do it and why it was better to do it in that way. Naturally we did it that is we tried to do it we were not at all good and we did it again, and again and again and he was patient helpful and charming. His name was Keane.

We drilled from eight to twelve in the mornings and after the first three weeks our feet and ankles gradually became less sore and swollen from our unaccustomed boots until finally we could leave off bandages and ointment.

Later when we went for route marches the officer in charge of us was always most meticulous in having foot inspections and each foot carefully was examined afterwards. Nothing ever then was anything the matter with us but it is a curious thing I never do remember ever having had a foot inspection in the beginning when something was the matter with each one of us. Anyway we had to get it over sometime so and why examine it.

The cold was still intense and conditions though tolerable were not as comfortable as I had been used to and I began to feel ill and then one day I was ill. An ambulance took me to hospital. I was not very ill but I still was ill enough. It was the only time my body did not come to the rescue, it did do what it could but it could not no really it could not cope with everything at once.

Just now I must begin mentioning about our depot that anything I am going to say about it, and just now I am going to begin really telling about it is what happens when they say what evidence you give may be taken against you. They say so but evidence really that is British evidence is not to be taken against you, evidence is evidence is something to be considered and decided and what happens when if it did. What I am going to begin really telling you now is the way it happened to me. In being what I then was and that was a raw a very raw recruit what then seemed to be happening seems not the same now when after it has happened. It is like comfort and discomfort is a comparative thing and then food, later on I shall be doing food and feeding is like shouting and drilling when at the time it is awful and amazing it gets better and after a time it is accepted that is you are used to it and after a longer time you are so used to it you can even begin to miss having it and after a further time that is simply ages after you can then look back on it and believe you liked it.

Well really what it is I think is that war standards are not peace standards why should they be, they should not be but to begin with you apply your peace standards to war-time conditions and it takes some time to make the changeover and until you coalesce in compromise then naturally you feel more uncomfortable and more disturbed more displeased and more resentful than really you need to be. After all if you have a war what is coming to you has to come and then at the end of it you go into reverse to get back again to what you once were feeling. It is very complicated the adjustment is but it comes to all of us and has to be done. Really and truly there are probably just as many people who enjoy a war as they enjoy a peace, they may perhaps be different people but probably as many people do not say so but really and truly there are who enjoy a war just as much as a peace. It just is standards are different and theirs are different in times of disturbance and stress.

I must say now that our depot was a temporary one, a transitory one. It exists no more and what its identity was can now no longer matter. Gone with the wind as the girl said who sought adventure through her service. She made an adjustment and well anyway we all have our trials to bear.

Our depot was a temporary one and who was there is now no more. I repeat it because in trying to identify it it will only be wasting time.

When I came back from being ill and began my drilling again immediately every thing was different, we did not have sergeant Keane we had a man who shouted. He did not say anything he just shouted. I thought at first he had a defection in his speech and once as a child I had been in Hyde Park when a boy had come by in a pram deeply roaring. As a child they would not tell me what it was but I knew he was a mad one. I was fascinated but shocked. This man we had was just like him. In a way it was fascinating and shocking and in a way also it was embarrassing, it was not quite nice. We marched up a hill, that is we rushed ten yards he roared we stopped. He roared we rushed he roared we stopped. He roared we rushed he roared we stopped he roared we stopped we rushed he roared we sweated he roared we rushed we stopped. It was dreadful.

Everything we did was wrong. He shouted and cursed he did not say anything he just shouted and cursed. He did not say what we did wrong or how we did it wrong, he just cursed every thing we did was wrong we did it again and again it was wrong. It was dreadful.

We became not interested any more in what we were doing. Why be interested in being wrong.

Before the war was declared it was often I was meeting young men who were seeing me to be given a job in the work I was doing if it was possible. It was not possible. I asked them why it was they did not join up in one of the services. Their answer was always the same they would not be shouted at. Their fathers had been in the war before this war and they had told them how they had been shouted at and that really I do think that was really how the war had affected them most that their fathers had been shouted at. It was not nice nor decent. Fighting and killing suffering endurance friendship courage and dying their fathers had had and now they their sons have had, they do not shirk it indeed they are glorious in it, but being shouted at they would not have. It is not the fear of it they have it is the humiliation. It is shocking and embarrassing and it is shameful, not for them so much but for the ones shouting it is shameful it is not quite nice nor decent. It is not the fear it is the shame and humiliation of it, and that is why shouting is so stupid and harmful because it is humiliating and humiliation is a wounding of the soul.

Shouting and ordering is not the same. Ordering is saying simply something must be done, shouting is not saying anything it just is shouting.

Drilling is difficult because it is simple because it is, and it is difficult because it involves discipline leadership and character, and it is the connection between them is what is so difficult and now that shouting and ordering have come into drilling it is even more difficult.

We soon went away to France, as I said once away we became sane because sanity was required and indeed it was taken for granted. We forgot all about the roaring mad drillers and then we came back and suddenly there they all were and as we had left them. Only inevitably to maintain themselves they were more so than they had been when as we had left them. Much more so. We were appalled. We did not mind about them but we did mind about the effect they were having on everyone else. Everything was repression punishment and suppressed chaos. Everyone shouted everyone cursed and everyone hated every one and every thing. I seldom am angry but this made me angry and after what we had been through with everyone being so kind and unselfish and every one helping everyone coming back to this made me absolutely angry. Stupidity backed by authority is more than an evil, it is a positive evil. It is inescapable, it is contaminating, it is devitalizing. It breeds despair it saps hope it fosters hatred and resentment it dulls the intellect it coarsens the mind it thickens the wearied body and it kills response.

How much worse it grew I do not know. We were sectioned off and posted to our stations. It did grow worse and naturally because stupidity is a form of power and if nothing will control it then it naturally grows worse. And stupidity being also weakness it has to have greater and bigger stupidity to make itself stronger. It is a very shocking thing.

The shouting cursing men upbraided roared and raved. That was our depot. Thank God it is no more.

That was what happened, it was difficult and is it important. Well yes it is important, it is important to feel that what you are in is like drilling and discipline is the best way of doing anything with ability. Surely it is important to feel you are a part of something with ability and that something is the best something that can be done with ability. I should hope so.

What is it then we are part of that something that is should be done with ability it is called Field Security and what does it mean.

It means well for one thing it means there never is enough of it, I mean by this there never is enough of anybody available for doing it it is surprising in a way not when you know it no it is not. Anyway they always say they want more doing it and more for training for doing it for they can not get enough for doing Field Security. For Field Security in its modest way is important.

They want most men between twenty-five and thirty-five who can speak one language at least one other language other than French and who do as well do have some character and who besides this do also have some sense of responsibility. Then too it is important what parents they have had, I think it is less important what wives they have had but about their parents it is absolutely important for them each to be a British one. If not who knows.

First before joining we were interviewed, we had a language test and we were looked at and ofcourse we filled up a form about who we were and what we had done and I think we gave references. Then after a suitable interval they said we might join them and if we were still available we did. Every one asked everyone what was Field Security and about ten recruits said oh do you not know we said no they said oh well if you do not know it is secret.

Then we asked those who were there what it was we had joined. Those who had been there not very long said it was secret, those who had been there quite some time said it was common sense, and those who had been there just too long said they had not the least idea.

After some weeks of drilling we did in batches what is called the Course that is a series of lectures lasting a fortnight and the lectures told us what Field Security is and is like. The lectures were so secret that any notes we made were locked away and at the end of the course they were carefully burnt and the ashes well stirred in the presence of an officer. As I never can remember anything that has not actually happened unless I have some notes to remember it by I cannot remember anything about the lectures. Anyway when the notes had been burnt they published an article about them in the press so everybody knew what Field Security was if what they said it was and it was to encourage them to join it. In 'My First War' a book of notes about Field Security and how it works in action the author says "my job was to thwart enemy attempts at espionage sabotage and propaganda" and I think that is what anyone may say that that is a fair comment.

The chief thing I remember about the lectures was I had a temperature of one hundred and the other thing was that during them we were not shouted at. The lecturers were good ones and everything was very sensibly arranged and now everything has been moved elsewhere from where it was and everything I am told that everything is very well arranged.

We had three exams in the fortnight of the Course, we had marks for them and if we did not get enough marks they said we were not security minded and it was rather awful not being security minded. There was a man there who spoke Russian Turkish Arabic Hindustani Hungarian French German Italian English and read wrote and spoke Chinese but he was not a bit security minded not in the least little bit. The only thing he could do really with certainty and reliability was peeling potatoes and he did do this and when he did not he sat and read Chinese in a far off corner of the gymnasium. Well.

Two things the first lectures wanted us particularly to know were not security was spying and blackmail. We had thought perhaps it was the one or the other or perhaps it was a combination of both because it was secret and war time secrecy is almost always spying and blackmail or huge munition dumps or a tiny laboratory with scientists in it who blow themselves up for the sake of whatever it is they are perfecting is tremendously secret, but we were not scientists and security was not spying and blackmail. Whatever people called us we were not spies and we were not gestapo. This pleased us all. Later when people said we were in fact gestapo we did not mind because we knew we were not because anybody does not mind being what he is not when everybody says he is if he is not. Well anyway we were not gestapo and we are not. People also called us then they said we were police, we were secret police or security police or any way police and we are not that either. To begin with in our training we were in the barracks of the military police and the military police did not like that at all naturally it was confusing for them to be confused with us and naturally they did not like that at all. They still do not like that at all. Anyway we very soon left the military police and we are not police. We are rather negative really, that is preventive we are not disciplinary we are protective.

To go back to spying and what they said about spying and the blonde ones doing it they said what the blonde spy was doing was a lovely dream. They gave a lecture explaining it all, the trouble they said is the demand is too great it exceeds the supply, there never are enough blonde spies to go round it is most disappointing but it can not be helped. We all laughed good naturedly to conceal our disappointment but of course it was most mortifying and those who were reading their Bernard Newman were returning it to the lending library as though they now knew it was fiction. Still illusion dies hard, there always is hope and I think we have all of us met at least one good blonde spy and if not why not it was not for want of trying, no it was not for want of trying.

That was blonde spies. They taught us too to think of spies as agents and we did so, we became quite serious as we thought of spies as agents and enemy agents is quite a different thing to blonde spies when they lose their glamour they become more purposeful. An agent really has no glamour, he might be anyone and if he is it is very disappointing, there always is enough of anyone.

Well anyway.

Security is mostly taking precautions against the possibility of damage happening to what should be secure. When the first security sections went out to France the precautions they took were if not damaging at least appreciably disruptive. They tested the security of any offices they found. What guards there were they satisfied or evaded, they entered the offices and took away the files and documents typewriters plans maps codes ink pens rubber stamps and the general's blotting paper. There was a fearful to do. Anyway having done it once was enough. The offices were secure from then on and the generals security minded. They said they would not draw positions of the gun emplacements on their blotting paper any more. Anyway they said so.

Mostly security is preventive. It is not aggressive nor colour-ful, nor conspicuous nor adventurous nor heroic nor glamorous nor thrilling nor very positive nor very defined. Mostly it is not. It mostly just is something that has got to be done in case if it is not done what should be secure would be not left quite as secure. It really just is that prevention is better than cure.

I think it is Maupassant has a story about a cockerel why does he crow at sunrise. He crows because he never can be sure that if he did not crow the sun would rise. Some times he does not want to crow and some times he does not feel it necessary to crow but when the dawn comes always he thinks how awful it would be if the sun could not rise because he did not crow. So always he does crow and the sun does rise. The sun as every one knows never sets on the British Empire and it would be just as awful if it did not rise. So well security is like the cockerel, it never can be sure if it did not crow that the sun would rise so it goes on crowing so the sun will rise. And well yes the sun does rise.

After the lectures those who have the fewest marks are sent for and those who have the highest marks are sent for. No one knows which and I was sent for. It was very amusing. We had just had a lecture on interviewing suspects how you interrogate them with your back to the wall and the light on their faces. I sat down facing the light they stood round their backs to the wall, four of them. They said was I liking what I was doing I said hastily oh yes. They said, well anyway they asked me all the questions I had filled in the answers to on the form some months ago so I knew they knew all the answers it was just a game. They said about the management of men had I done it and could I do it. I said yes. They said could I take a squad of men I said take them where to. They said drill them. I said probably not.

They looked at the form with the answers on, they said this hotel you were running was it large. I said no. They said how many could it be holding I said two hundred they said oh was it expensive I said not in the least for what they were getting they said how much I said seven guineas to start with and they said oh you mean it was first class. It was very amusing.

They still were worried about the management of men. They said what staff did you control. I said well when we were empty we had thirty-five and then later we had eighty-five and then ofcourse there were extras and ofcourse more extras for banquets and things like that. They said did you have any trouble with your staff. I said oh no I like staff, I always have liked staff they are so human they came back year after year and yes really I liked them, I would do any thing for them and they did everything for me but the visitors were awful. They said indeed. Ofcourse this was the wrong answer. There is what is called the servant problem, everyone has it it is really the employers problem but they call it the servant problem to make it sound more virtuous. Anyone who is anyone has a servant problem and I had not. It was quite the wrong answer.

They said what games do you play. It was very amusing. I knew what I was going to say and now I knew what they were going to say. They said what games do you play and I said tennis. They said we mean cricket and football. I knew it for naturally it happens to everyone that there comes a time when they say we mean cricket and football.

All this had happened to me before, I had forgotten but it was coming back. At my school on the syllabus tennis was one of the things included in the fees which you paid extra for, there was a court at the back of the house I was in and each summer term they came round and said if anyone wants to play tennis and if he does he will know the reason why, tennis is a girls game and don't you let us catch you doing it. So each summer term we stood in some long grass for three hours four times a week and that was cricket and like Guinness it is good for you. Well anyway here I was back again, the interviewers did not say tennis was a girls game but it worried them. It did not rank as a game quite clearly not, cricket and football are games, swimming and boxing are sports, golf is a hobby, polo is a privilege, shooting hunting and fishing are social exercises. Well anyway that is the code. I said I played tennis because I liked it. This was as disappointing as having no servant problem.

They then said what are your interests. I said, well I now was suspect and why not tell them. I never have much minded what people think I am, what bothers me much more is what I think of them. I said my chief interest is music. There was a short silence. They were very polite, very courteous, and slightly embarrassed. The interview was over.

Those who were passed as eligible were promoted to the rank of unpaid acting corporal and proceeded to embark upon the management of men. They went about in pairs, the pairs then parted, each half stood apart two hundred yards from the other half, one half shouted, the other half shouted back and there they were. Then the shouting back one shouted and the other one shouted back. They went on shouting until either they grew hoarse or they used up the shouts they had been given to shout out. Then the one who knew all the shouts to be given came round and gave them new ones to be going on with and in this way so it went on.

Well anyway if the management of men is a science why not.

The days dragged on, Monday followed Sunday, and then gradually arrangements were beginning to be made. We were given equipment and we went out marching in it, then we were given more equipment and we went out marching in that. Monday followed Sunday and we were being taught motor cycling.

The peculiarity about the young man who taught us motor-cycling was that everything was bloody. It was most peculiar how every single thing was bloody. The bikes were bloody the tools were bloody the oil was bloody and we were bloody and I was bloody. It was very peculiar. When I fell off as I did quite often I was exceedingly well bruised but luckily not bloody. The young man said I was absolutely bloody. Was he a nice young man I do not know.

One day I went into a place when I saw him eating there. I had never seen him before. He was always covered up in goggles gauntlets helmets leggings and rubber boots and water-proof jerkins because in motor cycling it is requisite to have the protective paraphernalia which appear to be the common property of motor cycling and baseball. I do not know why but I think it is that motor cycling and baseball are the two things most alike which do necessitate most violence mud and tumbling. Anyway he was eating and I saw him eating there. He was very young, with pale clear skin fair hair and blue eyes. I was astonished. Suddenly I knew how fearful it must be to have to exercise authority with only one adjective to do it with. Poor young man. Perhaps he was a nice young man I do not know but I know he came from Birmingham.

So Monday followed Sunday, the days dragged on and then we were to go. Everything was arranged. We were equipped and inspected and re-equipped and inspected and again inspected and inspected again and again inspected. Everyone was inspected every thing was inspected, we were counted and re-counted, marched backwards and forwards, in and out round and about, we turned about, we saluted on the march, we formed threes, we had pistol drill and gas drill and physical drill. Every possible fault was found and every possible punishment devised.

We peeled potatoes washed dishes scrubbed floors cleaned lavatories dusted offices carried coals polished pen nibs with brasso. Everyone shouted and ordered and counter-ordered. We were divided up into sections, we were given a sergeant, and then a sergeant-major and then we were given an officer. We moved our bedding and moved it back again and we were divided up again and we moved our bedding again and we slept in the gym and we were to sleep on one side and then not it was the other side and more sections came in and we were divided up again and we were in different sections and then we were to sleep in the middle and then not we were to sleep at one end and we moved everything from one end to the other end and then not they said we were to sleep at the sides and well anyway we were in a coma. Monday followed Sunday we were to go we were not to go, we were not to go and we were to go. We packed and unpacked, repacked unpacked packed and packed. And everybody ordered and shouted and ordered and counter-ordered. Finally we did go. I have said so. We were utterly dazed.

So now we were in a rest camp at Southampton. It gradually dawned on us that what we had been through was not the army but what the army might be if it went mad. But then thank goodness the army is not mad, not always mad and never not as mad.

It was still and peaceful sitting still under the tree in the garden. A bank of crimson rhododendrons glowed warmly in the evening sun. There was a scent of pines and cedars in the air. It grew dusk. I got up and walked into the house. The others were coming back. We spread our ground sheets on the floor and undressed and lay in our blankets on the boards.

It was our first night of freedom. I slept soundly.

3 Crossing

The buses came to the door. We got into them with all our equipment. They drove us down to the docks. We got out and marched some distance. It was very hot with our full equipment on our backs and we had our bedding to carry and other things besides. We came to the side of a ship. We were counted over and given a life jacket each and a paper bag containing two large meat pies, an apple a banana a roll of bread and a packet of cheese. We walked up the gangway on board.

The ship was crowded. We found places in a passage, just our Section thirteen of us, and put our equipment there and sat on it.

More and more soldiers kept on coming on hundreds of them. Long lines of them moved along the quay towards the waiting ships and filled them fuller still. I found a canteen and got some coffee. I went up on deck. There was a sense everywhere of anticipation excitement and adventure.

The soldiers were eating out of their paper bags. We had had a meal in the rest camp at half past eleven, it was now about three. I ate a meat pie.

The organization was very good. There was no shouting pushing fussing ordering and counter-ordering. Everyone was treated as though they were sane and adult and this was enough to make them so. We were still not yet used to such treatment and it gave us all a continuous pleasure and a pleasure to be alive. Everyone was very cheerful, not boisterous but just happy.

The ships moved slowly out of harbour. We cruised gently down Southampton Water for perhaps two hours and then stood still. When darkness fell we were to move across the Channel escorted by destroyers.

It was lovely cruising down Southampton Water. The sun was brilliant the sea was blue and everything on shore was clear and visible. The barrage balloons were very high and very silver in the sky. We passed much shipping and once we saw a submarine. It was said to be on trial. We watched it for a long time slinking along around us. It was a fascinating sight the long grey shape moving so swiftly silently slinking along the surface of the sea. It was low and close to the water lying on it and stretching itself upon it, it was like the water had conceived it. It was beautiful, and disturbing. It gave the impression of soft and secret power, like a blue grey orchid poised upon the sea. It was fascinating. It did not submerge it just went.

I stood by the rail on the top deck. I was very excited. I wanted to laugh. It was happening at last and it was happening to me. I was on a troopship going to France. It was so impossible, so absurd. I wanted to laugh. I wished my family could see me how they would have laughed it was so impossible. It was like being what you see on the news reels in the films, you always see numbers of people on them quite ordinary people but you never do see anyone you know and you never do see you. Well anyway here I was one of some thousands of troops on a troopship going to France and there was a war on and I was a soldier. It was not possible it was happening to me.

It was funny. We that is my generation could remember the last war in our feeling of it and had grown up under its heated noonday shadow. We that is in its heating we were growing and our consciousness was growing up and in its fearful aftermath it had grown up but already it was formed. When it ended, that is when an armistice was made it did not end it just stopped the fighting just stopped the rest went on, I was thirteen and I have often been surprised my mother saying I did not remember it I was too young. I was not too young and none of my generation was too young and none of this young living generation is too young to remember what war is in their feeling of it. In their feeling they are growing up and already in their feeling they are being formed. It is very important this feeling of it what this war has been and means. Dates facts casualties numbers and locations and the ebb and flow of war matter only at the time of war and then only for those directing the major operations of war, that is others feel them as they matter to each one but they do not understand them and they can not comprehend them they can only feel them and this makes the difference of war for those in war and those coming after one that those in war can not comprehend the magnitude as those who coming afterwards can understand the significance of the numbers and locations of the major operations of a war. They can not understand it they can feel it and they only comprehend it in its aftermath when their feeling has been formed. But their feeling is forming and growing each generation in their feeling of a war is being formed and this young living generation already in their consciousness this war is being formed.

It is very important and very interesting the difference of war for those in war and those who just come after one and my generation do know this difference after first coming after one and now being in one. The difference is interesting that now we know it. In the feeling of those who come after a war there is chiefly the horror and sadness of it. My generation certainly felt the horror and sadness waste and futility of war and felt them very deeply. But now my generation who are in a war what is it we feel most deeply is not the horror and waste of it but the honour and nobility of doing it, not my generation only ofcourse but every generation in this war feel the honour and necessity for this war, the horror and waste yes a little sometimes there is grief and sorrow of those who have lost whom they cherish but the chief feeling of honour and necessity engulf this grief feeling of sorrow and loss, we will fight on the beaches on the hills and in the villages for our honour and our glory it is very important and yes it is disturbing. It is disturbing that war has come to be felt to be more noble and worth while fighting for than peace had come not to be felt to be worth while living for. It is disturbing but it is perfectly true that which of the two is more honourable and noble September 1938 or September 1940, the peace with honour as Mr. Chamberlain said or the Battle of Britain as Mr. Churchill said. It is not surprising to us who are in it but it will be disturbing to those who come after it. Perhaps the living young generation now beginning their feeling of it will not be like my generation not feeling the horror and sadness of war but will always be feeling the honour and glory of it and remembering the shame and fear and the dreadfulness of peace. It is important for them and it is important for us what they will be feeling for war and for peace. Is it for them to say that we were wrong or for us to show them what was wrong.

It is curious to feel that my generation erred in their feeling that war was so wasteful and wrong. Is it so.

It was funny. My generation who have known the last world war in our feeling of it have never known what peace is like. There has always in our memory been trouble and fighting and revolutions insurrections and invasions and civil wars going on somewhere, always someone and large numbers of someone have been suffering and oppressed. In Europe in Asia in Africa there has been a constant struggle of humanity, ebbing and flowing, right and left, inarticulate confused, always struggling for something. It is not yet defined. In America they have called it names, like depression, unemployment, supply, demand, financial speculation, over-production, economic dislocation, everyone has called it names and other names, like capitalism, socialism, communism, fascism, naziism, and democracy and dictatorship, but it is not. It is not anything like politics, it is deeper much deeper than politics are not deep it is a very curious fact that having universal suffrage has meant for every-one that politics can matter much less than before. The struggling for something is not political and it is not articulate, it is not yet defined.

My generation knew that in its feeling of the last world war that the struggle had begun. It almost seemed that afterwards it might perhaps be defined and they tried to define it but it could not be defined. Perhaps it can not be defined. It is growing. It is not formed but it is growing it is not articulate but there is a feeling for it that it is growing and that in growing that it will evolve and come.

After the last world war they wanted it to go back to what it had been but it does not go back it does not begin again, it is very complicated to begin again. It mostly does not happen until there has been a good deal more destruction. After this destruction we will we must begin again.

Anyway I stood on the deck and I wanted to laugh. And

everyone on board the troopship was excited and happy and everyone wanted to laugh and we all did laugh. It seemed to us natural to do so. War, being in a war, is a very funny thing.

They were serving out tea and bread and iron rations down below. We stood in a queue. The queue went right round the ship three times.

Everyone began lying down for the night. I went up on deck. It was cool up there but healthy. Every corner was occupied. I found some place, it was on top of some thing sloping down. People came round to stop our smoking and every thing was very still. It was midnight. It was quite dark with a starry sky. I could see some dark shapes on the sea. They were destroyers four of them, French ones. The night was very still, the waves just lapping us and cool sea breezes touching us as we lay in our places waiting for the anchored ships to move. In the small hours of the morning we began to move quite quietly, four troopships and four destroyers French ones. We glided darkly through the night across the English Channel.

When we started I found an empty seat and lay down on it in my clothes and great coat with a blanket over me. It was very cold. At five oclock I went below to get a shave. There was a huge queue stretching from the cloakroom door right round the ship the tail meeting the head. I found some coffee and joined the queue.

By half past seven I was in the cloakroom and the ship was entering Le Havre.

We disembarked. There had been no incident in crossing. I suppose that when the war is over some laconic announcement will be made that so many hundred thousand troops and hundred thousand vehicles were shipped across the sea without the loss of a single one. And everyone will accept it as quite natural and proper. And yet consider the organization required, the planning the dovetailing the assembling, the consultation and co-operation and consideration of all the different authorities involved, not only that but the doing of it all in secrecy and security.

I thought it was significant that in spite of all the complications inherent in our transportation someone still had time to think of all those thousands of paper bags of food for the troops. It would have been sufficient to have given us our midday meal and the tea and bread on board. But someone had found time to think of all those paper bags, at the right time in the right place in the right numbers. Most people do find it a fearful nuisance to pack up a picnic lunch for six. But up to sixty and six hundred what the British army does for its men does not let them be a fearful nuisance up to six thousand and six and sixty thousand. I think this thoughtful touch did give us all a feeling of assurance that come what might we would not be forgotten.

We disembarked.

PART TWO: THE ARRIVING

4 *Le Havre*

We walked off the ship and assembled on the quay, and immediately there was an air raid. We lay under the wall of a building. We heard the guns and watched the puffs of white smoke bursting over the clear blue sky. The enemy planes were on reconnaissance. They had a good look at us and then flew away.

After the raid had begun we were surprised to see a number of barrage balloons climb up into the sky. One quite near us was being slowly raised. The crew had been at breakfast. It was a little surprising. I think now it was a little significant.

After a while we walked some distance through sheds and yards carrying our equipment with us. It was very hot. Then we walked all the way back again. We had each been given another blanket to carry. We now began a period of long waiting for our motor cycles to be unloaded. They were hoisted by cranes from the hold over the ship's side on to the quay two at a time in steel mesh baskets. Each man took his machine and strapped his equipment on the carrier of it. All our possessions, that is everything we had was carried in this way on the back of our bicycles.

We walked the machines off the quay to a filling station for petrol. We were given fuel enough for a short journey and we were given directions to a central car park and set off driving through the town. We remembered to keep to the right of the road. We reached the car park round about one o'clock. This was to be our home for the next few days.

The car park was a large place. It was the sort of place that all towns having it the municipal authorities try to conceal. It was where whatever noone wanted was sent to accumulate to be destroyed. There were piles of it round the edges of it. A gasometer and a factory looked on. Everything else in the car park was British. There were cycles and cars, lorries vans trailers and various types of guns. After a shower of rain the entire area became a liquid sea of deep black mud. It was dry now, we bounced over the ruts. We parked our cycles in rows, together, in Sections.

At one end of the place stood four Nissen huts. These are those circular ones with the corrugated roof sheeting coming down to the ground on each side of a wooden flooring, the circular ends boarded up with a door through each end and a stove stands in the middle. About twenty men lie down each side their feet to the centre, there is not much room for them and much less room for their equipment. However we got in where we could.

Almost immediately we had a meal. There was an arrangement of cooking stoves in the open at the back. We went out with our billy cans. We had stew and a packet of biscuits margarine and jam and some warmish bacon in a tin, we took these back again into the Nissen hut and sat down in our places on the floor and ate it there.

It was very interesting. We had not used our billy cans before and we now had army biscuits for the first time too. It was like being soldiers. A billy can is very interesting till you get used to it and then it is useful. It is a bottom lid with a top one fitting inside and each with a handle. The bottom being larger and slightly deeper is used for stew bacon baked beans cleaning rags letters two Penguin books potatoes shaving water and anything else useful and nice to have. The top one is used for jam and biscuits margarine drinking tea and for lending to those who have lost their bottom parts. The billy can shuts up and fits into a linen bag which is used for holding all odds and ends and anything loose like sparking plugs and string screws foreign currency boot polish and so forth.

We noticed how all the hotness in the food went into the handles. It was interesting at least it was interesting to us.

Army biscuits are a lasting pleasure. I found them delicious. There are two sorts thick ones and not as thick ones. The not as thick ones are very pleasing and sustaining nourishing and helpful. You can eat more of these than any other biscuit without feeling thirsty and you do not need to eat a great many before you feel you have had a meal. But then you can eat a great many without becoming tired of them. Well anyway I could. I saw a great many and I ate a great many in France in England I have never seen nor eaten any not one.

We were all paid that afternoon in French money.

I began now to do the duties of a clerk for our Section. There are thirteen men in a Section ten lance corporals two sergeants and a sergeant-major and then a driver and also an officer. I will ofcourse come to all these later just now I am just beginning.

I think we were three days in Le Havre or perhaps it was four, I have no recollection of three or four or of any of them. I think we had a parade in the morning and the rest of the morning they told us to overhaul our machines. I think we had then lectures what to do when our machines did not if they did not like the overhauling they had got. As I never have the slightest idea of what a machine does do or how it does it I never either have the slightest idea of what or how to do it when it does not. Mostly I find machines do not and I think motor bicycles particularly do not anyway when they go they usually stop and when they stop they sometimes go and what decides the issue is I do not know.

In this way the time passed on without it seeming to be going or coming. We were not yet used to being free. We felt rather like the people in the ghetto in Mr. Chaplin's film The Great Dictator, we always expected everything to change back suddenly to roaring shouting and terror and to hear the mad driller not saying anything but just shouting. Gradually we got used to it not happening any more but I think some of us were still listening out for the noise and shouting to begin again. It takes some time to remember and just as much time to forget.

Anyway they did their machines in the car park and I did my clerking in the Nissen hut.

It was strange being in France like this. We knew we were in but it was not like being in, everything around us was British, where we slept what we ate what we said was perfectly British. The only thing French were the sounds around us. It always interests me the every day sounds of every country are different and peculiar to that country. Trains and trams but particularly trains are always different sitting in a train from England to Italy is quite a different sound in France and Switzerland and in London and in Naples it is different. The sound of motor horns is exceedingly different and carts along streets and the shoes of people walking are different each in their country makes their sounds sound different. Just recently I was in a train going from England to Scotland and a young man in it when it started said ah listen when the engine makes that sound I know it means Scotland. It did and it is interesting.

We went up into the town in the evening, we had an apéritif in a café in the central place, I had a coffee I do not like apéritifs they do not interest me, the coffee was not very good and the others said, they did not say their apéritifs were very good so we went to a big restaurant with bright lights marble tables and red plush sofas, it was said to be a good one gaily populated and a popular rendezvous of Le Havre but it was not very good, there was nothing very bad it was just not very good. I was not very interested I am often quite easily not interested, noone was very interested and noone was very interesting we had hors d'oeuvres tournedos with salad and I think it was a Clos Vougeot and macedoine of fresh fruit and coffee and liqueurs, it was quite good and noone was very interested. We walked down back to the car park.

Something, there was something I was working out. Something had started it, I did not know what, I do not like to be bothered when something has started something I like to be able to clarify it. The Nissen hut was very crowded, everyone had been out and now they were coming back and none of them had had Clos Vougeot or if they had it had interested them to have more of it than some of them could deal with. Two men on the other side opposite me were saying what they always do say in that state about women and it really is extraordinary how uninteresting such men always are when they say is what they always do say about women in that state. Well anyway the man in the next place to where I was was undressing and in taking off his things was putting them down on all over me, I explained I said it was not his clothes which were moderately supportable but if he would move his equipment off me it would be an agreeable gesture much appreciated. He seemed completely surprised.

Eventually we settled down for the night and then it was remembered there was no guard over the machines in the car park outside. Two men had to go on guard and then two more to relieve them and two more in two hour shifts to relieve them. The going and the coming ones made it difficult in the Nissen hut it was pitch dark and it is difficult, being stepped on all over always is difficult, it was not a very settled night we had.

Something had started something and I wanted to clarify it, it was something to do with Le Havre but also more than Le Havre. It was worrying. It was something to do with the war and the French way of making war was not the British way it was worrying. In England ofcourse we had left England at war, nothing had happened and noone much minded. London was the same, everyone appeared to be the same and really everyone very much was the same. In war and peace there was practically no difference and why should there be since nothing had happened to make any difference. Everyone knew there was going to be a difference, they were quite prepared for a very big difference but why should it make any difference in peace or war when nothing had happened to make that difference.

In France nothing had happened either but immediately there was a difference, everyone was making a difference and were having in their feeling a difference. In Le Havre and Southampton there was quite a big difference. It was worrying. The blackout was worrying, in Le Havre the blackout was hardly any of it. I went into a grocery to buy some chocolate and I asked them why they had no blackout, they said oh yes we can do it it is left to each one of us to do it if we like to do it. Some did like some did not like and that was the blackout. It was not serious but the war yes that was serious, everyone said it was serious or they did not say so they felt it was serious because war is a serious thing. Nothing had happened but it would happen. In Le Havre they were as serious now as they were going to be because they knew that war is a serious thing and if nothing had happened it was going to happen and when it did happen it was going to be serious.

It is hard to explain this thing that the French were feeling. They were feeling it I know they were feeling it. It worried me first in Le Havre and then I forgot it but underneath it was worrying and later on it was more worrying still. It is hard now not to feel that the worrying was not real but imagined because the catastrophe that has happened to the French has happened to them so much because they were having this feeling for the war of ominous foreboding. The more I think of what the French were feeling the more worrying it is because the feeling of a nation is not simple, it goes back and back and the French feeling what they really feel is not simple, their feeling is not consecutive like ours it is consecutive with interruptions which makes it not as simple. It was very worrying at first this feeling in Le Havre of what the French were having in their feeling for the war. It was not imagined. I did not go up into the town again, yes I did once again, I did not like it, I stayed in the car park and did my clerking. It is not nice to have these feelings, it is worrying.

Later on the French were feeling more foreboding and later on I will say so.

We did not know at all what plans there were for the future. It is curious in the army you do not know, you get so used to what you do not know that if anything happens or not you just wait for it, you do not wonder or expect it you just wait for it. We were waiting and the time passed on without it seeming to be going or coming. There were all the rumours that we were to go and we did not go and the rumours became like everything else if they started we did not. Then one morning they said we were starting and then not that morning but another morning we did start.

We left the car park in a long line of roaring motor bicycles. We felt that this that really this was really was adventurous.

We were going to some place near the Belgian frontier, I forget where it was anyway we were certainly going there.

Actually we never did go there, it always happens in the army that anywhere you are certainly going to you never do go there. We went to Arras.

It was a very long journey, it took ten hours. I remember two things, the immense amount of dust we made, we were coated thickly all over with dust right into our skin it went and I remember everybody's great clear happiness. It was pleasantly hot and sunny and a Sunday, every place we passed through there were people walking and they waved to us and we waved back. The French children put their thumbs up and we put ours up and the old men waved and we waved and the women stood and smiled and we rode past and smiled. Everyone seemed pleased to see us and we were pleased to see them. We were very happy and every where we went was happy too.

We had lunch in some woods. I looked for wood anemones but there were none it was warm but it was a late spring. We saw some wild daffodils though and once I saw cowslips, you can not see much in a convoy but I did once see cowslips, the wild daffodils were very pretty and a great pleasure. In the countryside in France having no hedges makes it wider and seeing more of it in a glance, you can not see much in a convoy and seeing it was very pretty and a pleasure.

We were all very healthy. We had all been living out of doors with plenty of exercise, plain food, early sleeping and early rising.

We reached Arras about six in the evening. Our officer went into a building and there was a long conference and at once the rumours started again. Anyway he came out and we were to follow him. By now the sixty of us were now no longer with us, they had gone their various ways in their different Sections, and now at Arras we were just our Section just the thirteen of us and our officer. He led the way and we followed.

It seemed a long way at the end of the day and we thought we were going to the Belgian frontier. We came to a very small village, the car turned into a farm yard, we were very astonished, we stopped and dismounted and we said where are we and they said this is it.

They just said this is it.

Later we discovered it had a pleasing name called Givenchy-le-Noble.

This was our headquarters for the next few weeks until we began our fleeing to the coast.

It was an impressive moment, we had arrived at our destination. We were at last on active service. And almost at once we went to bed.

5 *Givenchy 1*

Givenchy-le-Noble is a very small village not a pretty one. Quite flat it is and a little hill comes down each side of it and into it a road runs through it there is a second one bisecting it in the middle of the village and twenty small houses that is all.

A little way past the cross roads we had our office in a part of a farm house with the village shop attached and a barn and cow stables, there were two farm houses joined that is they were separated by a farm yard they were not adjacent buildings but the families in them were consanguineous ones there was Madame and her husband and her daughter-in-law and her son who was a soldier and they granted him agricultural dispensation so there was her son there and then their son a little one of five and a baby son I do not remember their names, the little son of five was Roger, he was the one who was grubbier than any other child had ever been and once he came into our office at a very secret moment he was asked to leave and he cried.

His mother the daughter-in-law cried too about Roger not but about the war yes she was always rather weepy about the war and poor France and the British who were always rich and had a navy how could they help poor France who had nothing, the Germans had everything and France poor France had nothing. Well anyway.

Madame was the one who did everything that is the daughter-in-law minded the shop she never made anything, everything came in vans bread and biscuits mostly and bottles of beer and bottles of water there were not many people to buy anything still there always was someone to buy something and she minded the baby and she minded the shop but Madame was the one who did everything.

Madame was a grand woman a grand old peasant woman not old in years but old in her wisdom and in her strength she was as old as France is old, her strength was like a deep straight furrow. She ploughed the fields and sowed the grain, she milked the cows tended the horse reared the pigs and calves and nurtured chickens killed hens did the cooking for the family and the washing and the cleaning and cultivated the vegetables in her garden. She rose at six in the morning and retired at eleven at night, she never stopped working and she never was cross or upset or disheartened and she found time always to make us coffee and give us butter and bread and do our laundry and wash our floor and she would put flowers in the room and she would say toujours du travail messieurs mais comme la vie est belle.

We were installed in our office it was the living room of the daughter-in-law had been when they married it had been re-decorated a new stove put in and so forth it was a pleasant little room with two windows, our officer sat by the one looking over the farm yard because anyone coming in he liked to see them first who it was and they came in from off the road into the farm yard and he would say here is soandso now what on earth can he want and if it was one of the Section coming in he would say good lord here is soandso now has he had an accident. I sat by the other one overlooking the garden and every thing was growing it was a late spring but everything was beginning growing there were peas lettuces beans and cabbages and pota-toes and peonies and moss roses. Madame came in one day and she said they think they have made me a salad of my lettuces but I will make of them a cold pigeon pie the damned beasts.

At the corner of the cross roads was the village café and we went in often I went in every night to get some food I had always oeufs sur le plat as they called them they were slowly fried in butter in a pan on the top of a stove and two pieces of French bread it is moist bread not like English new bread it is moist bread but it crumbles and with butter on it you can not spread the butter it is very pleasing it was pale white butter rather salty and white wine was sharp and rather rough, eggs bread butter and white wine I had them every evening they were simple and very pleasing and I liked them every evening. They cost about seven pence.

Up the road was another café which we did not go there it had a bad name and the military police went there. It had a bad name and it is curious how even in a very small place there always is a place for a bad named place and so the military police went into it often and I went into it once.

It was like it was shut up when we went into it I was with Pound. It was a dimly lit chamber a tiled floor and coats and hats hung up around it and a circular wooden bar with shelves and bottles behind it all shut up. We examined the coats and hats and the one we were wanting to be investigating his was there but nothing in the pockets and then we heard noises and laughter. We saw a thread of light coming under a door and a sound of smashed glasses and then more laughter the door opened and a woman came out. She was hostile but anxious. We said good evening she said what do you want we said a drink and she went back into the room and it suddenly hushed and she came out again. She said there are no drinks here we are closed I am sorry and good night. We said we thought we heard sounds like people were making when they were drinking, she said yes we are having a little family party for our son back home on leave and now good night. We said, well we said it as though we had just thought of it we said oh is it that you are thinking we are the military police how very funny and she said and are you not and we both laughed heartily we said how could we be the military police if we are both hiding from them. Oh she said oh well won't you come in.

We went through a door and immediately well everything was crowded and it was confusing let me see. Ofcourse everyone was drunk there were seven or eight British troops very drunk and there were some French civilians and then everything was champagne bottles. We were all sitting round a table and everything on it was champagne bottles, I think they said they had had forty and a bottle cost two and fourpence. Still forty two and fourpences of anything is a good deal. A man came in with an armful of bottles and everybody grasped one and off with its head and the foam splashed over the table.

The thing we had to do was to find out the man who was said to be saying secret things in the village. There was in the village an installation of great secrecy it was very large complicated and enormously expensive and if anything happened to the forces in

France it was said to be the very last link between France and Great Britain. It was hidden away somewhere and it was very secret and when we came to the village the villagers asked us, of course it was very surprising for them that a body of British troops on motor bicycles arrived all speaking French fluently so they naturally asked us what it was and we said we did not know, at that time we really did not know and then they told us what the secret installation was. They were very proud of having anything so secret and valuable in their village and so naturally it was a pleasure to them to discuss it and tell us. We did not believe them ofcourse not and our officer went to the officers mess and said to the engineering officer I say these villagers have some funny ideas about your installation and the engineering officer said by jove have they really, well as I do not speak one word of their bally lingo I do not know if their ideas are funny or not so our officer told him and he said oh yes by jove their ideas are quite right, ofcourse it is a bit technical don't you know old man but they have the right ideas whoever would have thought it in a little village like this by jove how awfully funny.

Well ofcourse being new to everything we were very much shocked. We did think what was secret would be secret. When we got used to secrecy we got to know then that the chief thing about it is believing noone else knows about it and in this way secrecy is maintained. Ofcourse whatever is secret someone knows about it and who does not know about it is just a question of numbers and that really is secrecy, it is a question of the numbers of who does not know it. Anyway we did at that time think that what was secret would be secret and who ever had said about the installation was a British one speaking French to the villagers and in making inquiries we found out which it was his name was Eric but that was all.

The man I was nearest to drinking round the table had drunk enough by now to tell me his life story. Every one was telling someone some part of his life story and the noise was fairly general and the champagne bottles popping at intervals but by listening through the general noise I could hear one saying his life story in a sort of French. I said to the drinking one nearest me boozing is not that one Eric over there I know his face but what is his other name, Parker he said without stopping his life story hi Eric he said this mucking bastard is saying he knows you, the mucking hell he does said Eric show me the mucking bastard muck his mucking walls. Well ofcourse it was the two and fourpences and they did not mean it so. I said hello is not your name called Eric Parker I have seen you somewhere before and what part of England do you come from. He said Rochester, I thought where on earth is Rochester and I said why that is my home town too and he said by Christ I knew I'd seen your mucking face before and I thought yes this damn village is so small you are going to see my mucking face again and he said how is Tony Marshall. I said oh he was very well the last time I saw him and he said was he hell the double crossing bastard done me down on the mucking dogs the lousy punt. I said well Rochester is a very fine place and I wish I was back in it right now and that did the trick, he went sentimental and drank more champagne and then his life story began. It began from when he ran away from home and what a struggle he had had and how he went to South America and there grew jute or something and the crop just naturally failed and there he was. He had very white teeth and was dark and handsome in a pleasantly lascivious way and really there was something rather nicely engaging about Eric and he went on telling me everything, it was a pity he was suspect he was very drunk and we did dear Rochester again and I liked Eric he had personality he was drunk and suspect and well anyway there it was. It was a long story.

The table was running with dripping champagne and the supply seemed quite inexhaustible. The woman who had come out to see us disappeared through a door and she came back again carrying more bottles in her arms. The French man there I think was her husband would disappear too through the door and reappear with more bottles. We were all sitting close round the table in the light of a paraffin lamp everybody speaking loud and now they were repeating themselves. One man fell with a dull thump to the floor and another one smashed a glass hard into pieces. Then two stood up leaning over to each other swaying angrily and one had a bottle in his hand raised, they began a fierce argument and the other one was too drunk to see what was happening, he had his head lowered and the man raised his bottle higher and a little higher and the other man lurched forward until his head was nicely in the right position, the man took a deliberate drunken aim and he raised his bottle for the final swing, it was a dreadful moment. Then the gravity of the crisis was conveyed to the others sitting looking on, there was a shout and a scuffle the bottle was seized and dashed to the floor and the incident was over.

I lit another cigarette.

Behind our circle the room was in shadow beyond the radius of the paraffin lamp. The bottle crashed and in following its course my eye had caught the outline of a shape in the room's dark corner. Now I looked again. Through the haze of our smoking I saw a large double bed dirty and crumpled and on it sitting up and staring in a fixed and frightened way two small children, a little boy and girl clasping each other, mute and petrified with fear. The woman with the bottles called out an oath to them and with a stifled cry they shrank and burrowed under the bed clothes and lay there stretched and shivering, more terrified of what they could not see but only feel and hear as the night wore on. Above them hung a crucifix nailed to the wall. It looked so sorrowful looking on. The drunken men were shouting and arguing and one was being violently sick.

I said we must be going and we went from that place.

I wrote my report out that night and the next morning about midday the sergeant-major came into the office and said did any of you go to that café last night and I said I did and he said anyone else and Pound said he did. The sergeant-major said well you can die only once but there are mighty painful ways of making the dying last. Just after you left, he said, the military police raided the place and caught the whole lot red handed and there is going to be a court martial but before that happens they are saying they are going to make you two look like a very particularly bloody coincidence.

Well ofcourse it was awful. We went down for lunch to the

place where we ate and Eric came in and sat down and it all was awful, they just looked at us in a certain way they did not say anything but yet they did say something and it was awful. It went on like this for some days and then it came to the day when they put them on a charge and that was still more awful and now they were saying things like double crossing gestapo spies and mucking wolves in mucking sheeps clothing and the one about harbouring mucking vipers in bloody bosoms was exceptionally awful.

Anyway there still was something still rather nice about Eric and when he got to the viper in his bosom one I said well you seem to have made yourself rather uncomfortable and what about a drink but not if you do not mind not champagne at two and fourpence and he did not mind. It was all all right and he told me his life story over again how his home was in Lichfield he had lived there all his life until he joined the army last year and what a change it was he had always been sort of like it was retiring and seclusive before. Another life story he had was I think the one I liked best he was born in Great Yarmouth and went to sea and he joined the Indian Army, they had lots of battles and you gave the Indian boys one anna or something to clean your boots with it was no trouble at all, then he had grown tired of having no trouble at all and just as he was retiring with a pension for life the war had caught him and here he was back in the breach again. I liked this life story the best because it was nice about India with its tigers colonels and dancing girls and the jungle with the groves of marigolds as he said. His real life story was well not as nice but still there really was something rather nice about Eric and that was the first job I did of Security there was a little more to it than that but never mind that.

The place where we ate was in a building of the chateau. The chateau was like any French chateau of a medium size that is it was approached by a long straight avenue of straight tall trees at the end of which it stood in very good proportions and in very pleasant taste. It was not a large chateau as large as a nicely sized English country house but the beautiful proportions of its

French grey stone lent it the dignity of an eighteenth century mansion. Inside it and as so often happens in French chateaux and indeed in French houses the proportions disappeared, the rooms were small and not very well planned and it was surprising there was hardly any distance between the front and the back it was a little disturbing to be walking in and nearly walking out again, it was disappointing to be baulked of solidity.

The chateau was the headquarters of a variety of army branches, a Corps of Signals was there and DADOS and DAQMS DAAG and things like that whatever they mean they are necessary to have in an HQ and then anything attached to an HQ, we were attached to this HQ and some military police called CMP and RASC and DR's dispatch riders, and then all the letters were censored at the chateau and they had a censor there, the officers took it in turns to do the censoring and they did the units that did not belong to them to make it more confusing in their reading and anything considerably confusing that made it necessary for discretion to be the better part of valour then the censor did it and propriety was preserved. Anyway everyone went to the chateau, they never could find it up its long avenue but anyway they went there and everybody met there and that was our HQ.

On one side of it there was a wall round a garden with a chapel in it and on the other side a similar wall round a courtyard and the buildings round that were the stables and the stables were twice as large as the chateau was, they were huge. The court yard was immense it did not look it but it was a big expanse of cobbles, the stables were capacious and over them were different apartments, it was like a warren where the servants had been used to having their being and living. We ate in one of these rooms, we climbed up a long steep flight of worn wood stairs on the bottom stair carved on it like it was a recess was a wooden privy and you passed it by up the stairs to our eating room one side and a room with a kitchen range in it on the other side. Beyond this kitchen room was another room and then another and in this way it was if you went on long enough you did come to the installation that was so secret if it had been.

It was like a warren these rooms up stairs and in a way you could feel all the generations of the servants there had been there and their families and all their being and living centering on the chateau and below the huge court yard where the coaches had been turning.

It was very dilapidated now. The room we had for eating in the ceiling was hanging down in the middle, we always thought it would come down but it did not it just hung there suspended over our heads like a lath and plaster Damocles sword. There were holes in the walls and flooring and we had four trestle tables and eight wooden benches and we were not very many at a time but always we were coming in in ones or twos and when we could, dispatch riders chauffeurs orderlies, the office staffs were more regular in their habits and we were not too regular in ours. In a dark corner stood a bucket and as we went out each one tipped off what he had left over in his billy can into the bucket and then another bucket with thick brown water in it each one rinsed out his billy can in that and what you wiped it out with after was a matter of chance. It was not a very pleasant dining room, there was the feeling in it that all the food and sweat of years had soaked their wasted presence into the wooden floor and plaster walls. I never really got over the feeling I was eating a dead man's dinner there.

Through a hole in the wall we could see another room and a woman would come up and open a door with a huge iron key and she would go in and there would be laundry there. It was a very big long room low with curving rafters and it had a cobbled floor, it seemed very strange to have a cobbled floor upstairs and had they made their cheese and butter in it pressed grapes stored plums and apricots and dried pears and apples and gathered in their wheat and grain, had all the women servants worked and talked and gossiped there in their living and being for the chateau and spied upon the footmen in their powdered wigs going about their business in the cobbled yard below. I do not know. The whole place had an atmosphere of being over lived in.

The food we ate was not very nice or perhaps it was that the circumstances militated against its seeming nice. I have since wondered often about its seeming nice or its not being nice because once they wrote from home saying you never do say anything about the food you are eating so I wrote and said what food I was eating and it was soon after that that it was being said that the Field Security people were being dissatisfied with the facilities that they were having. It was not quite true and I have since been wondering about it.

It is very difficult to know about food if what is not nice is nice. It is like discomfort really being a comparative thing and can it be worse yes much and food can be worse yes much. Being in hotels ofcourse I have been interested in food and feeding and having had so much of it I am not any more interested in eating it but I always am interested in how it is done and how it is served and I certainly am interested in seeing it is done and done well. When the first meal I had in the army I shall never forget it because I never had imagined any food could be served and done in such a way and I never shall forget it. That was high tea and for breakfast next morning there was fried onions and I shall never forget that, that you ate off the same plate the onions that the marmalade was with. Then there was the tea I never can bear sweet tea and it was sweet tea with the milk boiled in it in thick pint mugs. I never had imagined it and within a fortnight I was not imagining anything else and the food was good, ofcourse it was the same food as it was before I had imagined it and when I had not imagined it it was uneatable but when after I had imagined it it was good, yes very good this was at the military police barracks and the food was very good.

To go on a little. The kitchen arrangements were excellent I was very interested in them, they had big double sided ovens and electric baking ovens and grills for fishes and toasted cheese there was plenty of space and light everywhere and large deep sinks for washing pots and pans and different sinks for washing vegetables. It was very well organized, they had I think they called him a sergeant chef he was a new one they got in to cope with the increasing numbers and I was interested in him because naturally I know after having had so many of them if they are going to be good or not by the little small things that they do or do not. He was going to be good and he was very good. Then later when our barracks were moved from the military police to some temporary ones and we went back to them from France the food was not good it was astoundingly bad. It was interestingly bad because it was a constant surprise to be seeing how good quality food could be made so consistently bad, and ofcourse being bad it was wasteful. Every day an officer with a body guard came through the place where we ate, the body guard said Silence the officer said Any Complaints and noone said anything and he went out. It happened each day that noone said anything he went out for what could they say. The men in charge of the kitchen arrangements could never possibly have been in charge of a kitchen before and then everybody who was doing kitchen work was being punished for not doing some other kind of work so when they said Any Complaints whatever could they say. However they were temporary ones. So the food in the chateau was not nice in the conditions of our having it and it was here I learned the conditions of eating do not matter so much as I had supposed. I do wonder about this how bad the conditions do have to be before the actual food is affected by them and then for great numbers of men I am noticing how really the conditions do not affect them in their feeding and eating and in their enjoyment of the food that they are eating.

When they said that the Field Security people were being dissatisfied with the facilities of the food they were having I did wonder about this thing. I came first to feeling that the conditions of eating like the hanging ceiling and buckets in the corner and even the wooden privy were not the facilities of eating because we did not eat them and then it was I discovered that eating to anyone is not tasting it is swallowing and filling up a void. Ofcourse this is not a discovery any English man knows it and then looking at the English ones eating there I gradually came to see that for very great numbers of everyone eating is just eating. This particularly happens that eating is just eating that is it is swallowing when you cease to be buying it and that makes the difference between hotel and restaurant food and private house food that once you start buying it cooked you criticize it but once you cease buying it prepared you just accept it. You or your wife or your cook cooks it, you do not criticize it you accept it and ofcourse you do have to accept it. Ofcourse I have known this difference for a long time because in catering you do know all about peoples likes and dislikes their funny faults and prejudices and what they like in food is each one likes to think he knows best if he buys it cooked and at home he is quite happy with tinned soup overcooked meat and something sweet and sloppy in a glass bowl and perhaps that horrid little sardine thing on a strip of dry toast they call a savoury well anyway in the army we were having stew and potatoes and a pudding and for tea cold meat and bread margarine and jam and we did not buy it and eating was eating it.

To go on a little bit longer eating in the army on location, they call it on active service but location is a better word is always like picnicking and I think this makes it nicer than it really is, certainly I have liked it better on location than eating in barracks. In the room with the range in it up the wooden stairs were three men cooking and it was not like a hotel kitchen they were in brown overalls and they did yes they did look like mechanics. The one who did the stews and he did them very well yes I will say that he often did them very well and pastry was a young one and I was told he had learned all his cooking in the army, he had never done any before and then he had volunteered to do it and so he had done it. He was a nice young man very pleasant and he looked like a mechanic, the three of them came to the café each evening where I was having my oeufs sur le plat and they had a glass of beer and talked about football and when the time came they would go out quietly and regularly. I never did know what had made him volunteer to do the cooking why he liked it but he did, he was a likeable young man.

Just the other day we were sent a book of army cookery with recipes and quantities and how to do everything for from one to one hundred, it is called a Manual of Military Cooking and Dietary and it says the information given in this document is not to be communicated directly or indirectly to the press or to any person and it is a pity that it is not. It is very interesting and there is something about it entirely army that makes it what it is, you need have no knowledge to start with, it covers everything and afterwards there need be no excuse for not doing it properly. There are dinners for privates and dinners for generals and Christmas dinners and Reunion dinners and diagrams to construct an oven in the open out of bits and pieces of anything handy and there is everything in it you could wish to know about good plain cooking. It is all so good and simple and there it is, all the trouble and the thinking and the publication and the distribution have been done, it is so like the army that all the trouble and the thinking have been done and then they are delegated and what happens to them. There are seventeen simple and sensible ways of cooking potatoes but have we ever eaten any than the simply wet and boiled. And there are twenty-eight different ways of doing vegetables, simple and sensible too with Vichy carrots and macaroni with tomato delicious and so easy but who does have them, who has ever had them. What a pity.

So it was we had our eating in the chateau and every one liked his eating by swallowing it, they did not buy it they accepted it and they always had enough of it and there was always more of it if they wanted it.

After we had been some days in Givenchy our Section was allotted an area of France to cover for security and we each were given a station in it. This was a very happy business because we all were living and sleeping in our office on the floor and it was exceedingly congested.

The area we had was perhaps as big as Yorkshire or bigger or smaller, we had St.Pol in the north and Peronne in the south and Arras and Amiens were on the edges of our east and western boundary. We had the town of Albert to cover too and Hyland and Calthorpe-Newman were the first to be sent away.

Hyland was our sergeant and was very nice about it. As he said, anyone could really be our sergeant and it happened to be him we must not mind and we did not mind not in the least. At this time Hyland was still having trouble with growing his moustache, whatever he did it always would come ginger and being the rest of him black haired his moustache was worrying in its coming ginger. However he kept it and kept at it, then on a day much later when he was afterwards in Scotland he took it all off and everyone was pleased and we said whatever had he done it for, he said he had grown tired of having it, we said no we mean why had he ever grown it and he said well it gave him a feeling of manliness but now he was engaged to be married he would not need it any more. We were surprised but well bred. Anyway Hyland was a very nice sergeant and noone thought about it and he did not and it was as it should be.

Calthorpe-Newman was always the one who was most cheerful of any of us, whatever the circumstances were he was always most cheering and very amusing, he was very witty and underneath he was capable and reliable and dependable on. It happens like this often when people have great gaiety of mind and spirits they can afford to have them when their feet are planted firmly on the ground. And I think of any of us he spoke the best French, certainly the most fluent and he had the largest vocabulary, his speciality was French and he knew it intimately and well. We were a very homogeneous Section and everyone liked everyone more or less, probably more than less, there were no feuds or rivalries or anything tiresome and childish like that, and each one got to know each other one and it was all all right. But I think in a way that everyone felt that in Calthorpe-Newman if ever there had been a difficulty that he would have been the one to go to because his sense of humour would have placed it in perspective and his sound common sense beneath it would have faced the difficulty fair and square. He got on well with every one. It was for these qualities that he was chosen to do a difficult job in a civilian camp of French men which would necessitate the exercise of tact and humour. It was not an easy job and it was unhesitatingly agreed upon that Calthorpe-Newman was the best one fitted who could do it and achieve it with success and sureness and essential discretion. He accepted it cheerfully. On the second night he was there the camp was bombed he was killed. It was a tragic business.

Barnes went off to St.Pol in the north, Houdret to Peronne in the south, Morris at Frévent was in the middle and Norris and Crew at Bienvillers and Beaumetz each had an area to cover. France Pound Lovegrove and Wright covered areas nearer home and these stayed on in Givenchy that is they slept there reporting back from their journeys each night. I was in the office and our sergeant-major Laversuch was there and Parham the batman-driver and of course lieutenant Ashby our officer.

After Hyland and Calthorpe-Newman Barnes and Houdret and Norris Crew and Morris had been disposed of the rest of us France Pound Lovegrove Wright and myself were found billets in the next village to sleep there. This was at Manin, Wright and I slept in a pleasant farm house, France and Lovegrove slept in another and Pound in a third. Laversuch slept in a room next the office in which everything else was kept like our stores of anti-gas equipment and spare clothing and motor cycling accessories, Parham slept in the office during the day he would sit in the bedroom and clean equipment and polish things and he would like to take things to pieces and then he was the one who made glue and ink it was upsetting ofcourse and he made it again. The bed of Laversuch was a useful thing to spread the camouflage net over to fix the brown and green cotton leaves on it. It always smelt strongly of seaweed and tar. Then when anyone important came into the office to see our officer we would leave them to it and stay in the bedroom until the importance had worn off. So Laversuch's bedroom was a useful place to have and how he slept in it we never did know but he said he did not mind and perhaps he did not, he was too good natured and kind hearted to mind any thing if it was of any help to anyone of us. He was such a wonderfully good man all over. He is an officer now with a section of his own, and may they deserve their good fortune he was marvellous to us and we knew it thank him.

There was one other bedroom through a door in Laversuch's bedroom and that was where the calves did sleep. All animals have their habits and these calves had pretty permeating habits but really I suppose they could not help them. Next door were the pigs. Madame would loose them out each day and they would go running round the yard and she would know each one by its name and I think it was once Théophile did a permeation of his own and Théophile and the camouflage net was really was well more upsetting than the ink or glue had been, they always say that pigs are nice clean animals when you get to know them and we got to know Théophile and well yes it was clean after we had cleaned up after him but Théophile was certainly a very permeating little pig and the camouflage net was never quite the same not afterwards. Théophile was never quite the same either.

At Manin Wright and I had very good rooms. I am telling all our sleeping arrangements because I shall be telling them later on how they varied, these present ones were too good to last and they did not. I had a four poster bed with a chintz canopy over it and I did not know which to be more enraptured with the having a bedroom to myself or having sheets and a mattress. It was glorious. Then I decided the best of all was having a pillow, it really is much nicer is a pillow than rolled up clothes are never wholly satisfactory I think it is the buttons and the pockets anyway the sheets were glorious and then it was exciting very exciting stepping up into a bed and being off the floor. I could not sleep the first night it was all too much exciting.

So we were all settled down in our various billets and the daily work went on.

The first thing our officer had to do was to know every body and they call this making contact. It seemed exhausting and complicated. Anybody who was anybody or who thought he was anybody and in war it is surprising how many of them do had to be contacted and in this way it was possible to see the importance of what an officer was. Ofcourse there are some who are somebody anyway without their having to think about it but not all not at all. Anyway for a fortnight our officer went about in his austin car and each day he came back looking exhausted and complicated with the importance of everyone thinking they were someone and he kept a diary. In it was anyone who was contacted his rank and initials and the spelling of his name and what bit of the army he belonged to. It is a very curious thing that once anyone becomes someone and someone official his name and initials have an importance in their order and spelling which they never had before in their civilian habits, noone in my civilian habits ever spells my name with accuracy and I do not ever expect them to it is usually Glyn-Jones or something like that and I do not mind that not at all but in the army I am always spelled with punctilious accuracy and even that is not enough I am given a number I can never remember it but it is important that someone remembers it and it is always accurate. Well that is how it is with what officers feel about the importance of their rank and initials and order and spelling is very important to have someone feeling the importance of remembering it.

Anyway our officer kept a diary of anybody somebody and everybody he had contacted with the object of calling them accurately what it was that officially they were. And every little helps if it does.

Being the officer of a Field Security Section is not at all an easy thing oh dear me no. After all in a Field Security Section or in quite a number of them noone is really much more stupid than anyone else so being an officer is naturally not an easy thing why should it be. Our officer was naturally not stupid and so we were pleasing to him and he was pleasing to us yes very, yes he really was an extraordinarily pleasing person it is odd that some people are like that and some are not, some nearly are but they are not and that makes all the difference if they nearly are they are not. Well anyway Tim Ashby was and ofcourse is a very pleasing person, he has that engaging and elusive thing called charm and that made all the difference to us, it made all the difference to me because I was in the office and so was he. To begin with we were rather shy of each other. Then when the shyness wore off it made him feel ill and gradually he was ill and then one awful day he was taken away. He had jaundice. It did not matter what it was what mattered was he was taken away, well anyway it was an awful day. Did he know it.

The only alarming trait he had was an irrepressible belief in his Section's worthiness. It is very alarming to be thought worthy. He thought us worthy. Then he spread the idea and he thought the Cause was worthy. Ofcourse once you start thinking about the Cause you are much better off thinking about something else.

However once he had to give a lecture to some troops about security and he began writing it and then I went on with it typing it and it was very alarming how the Cause kept coming on in and being thought worthy. I took out the worthiness and put in the Polish campaign it was very interesting how the Germans had prepared every thing and I was very security minded and said what should be said about counteracting espionage sabotage and propaganda and it was a very good lecture and I typed it. Tim Ashby then went off and gave the lecture and when he came back I asked him how did it go, he said well he had forgotten to take the notes I had done so he had done it all out of his head. I made inquiries and they said it was just like a thing on Empire building it was a huge success, they had gone away feeling thoroughly worthy proud and happy and it was not in the least bit boring like security is having to keep their bowels open and their mouths shut.

Good for them and for him.

We gradually got into things and it came to it that the week revolved round the writing of the Security Report it had to be in at GHQ by Friday night and it was very prolonged and exhausting. To begin with by the time it was meant to be in we had usually not managed to borrow the typewriter this took some time. I think it was DADOS who most often obliged. We sent down the car to the chateau and it waited and it came back and it was empty. Then whoever it was who could start his machine went down on his motor cycle and he waited and if someone was feeling well disposed the typewriter would be placed in another car and driven up to our office and that would be all right and we would promise to return it in half an hour. This would be Thursday or Friday and we would grudgingly release it under growling protest on Monday or Tuesday. Sometimes it did happen that in the security we had been investigating we were led to inquire into provinces which had we been otherwise engaged would have remained as provinces to be treated with circumspection and reserve. In this way it did happen twice and once for some days that our sergeant-major was quite unable to appear himself in the sergeant-majors mess. It was very awkward. Then when we sent for the typewriter it came back not in a car but in a wheelbarrow and the wheelbarrow had been used for well for something else first it was very awkward. Nevertheless.

The Security Report was a review of the week's happenings in our area and it did not go to HQ in the chateau but to another HQ in another chateau, this was four miles away in a small country town called Avesnes-le-Comte. You will be hearing a lot about Avesnes-le-Comte. Anyway on Saturday they would telephone for the security report and say where is it what has happened to it and we would say they should have it now at any minute now a dispatch rider has it it is on its way. Then Ashby would read it through to see if it sounded as awful in the light of day as it did in the dead of night and if it did and it usually did he would slip in something worthy into the morale section. Then Wright would start up his motor cycle and away it would go to Avesnes-le-Comte and we would go to the village shop and buy biscuits and Madame would make us strong black coffee, and that would be that for a little while.

The security report was divided up into several sections or categories. I forget what they all were, there was espionage sabotage and propaganda ofcourse, and British troops' relations with French civilians and then the rather intriguing one about thefts of petrol and clothing, and the not at all intriguing and very wearying one about rumours, and then the category of French civilian morale and British military morale. Each man in his area sent in reports about any thing which would come under any of these categories and ofcourse if there was any thing else he reported that too. My job in the office was to record these reports, make a précis of each one, file it under its category and then be able to find it when it was asked for. Ofcourse it never was asked for but some small thing that was mentioned unobtrusively was always asked for so I then made a different system to find it when anything was asked for. This worked very well so long as they could remember what it was they wanted to find out. I suppose there were fifty or sixty reports in a week and then there were all the verbal messages and the telephone messages.

The weekly security report was a boiling down of all of them.

There are three things needed in a report, they are legibility accuracy and briefness. Ofcourse we were told all that in our training but it is a different thing knowing it and doing it. After a little practice I do think they all were very good in doing it and Laversuch once was so good, it was a very long and complicated report about leaflets dropping and it was particularly important because there was a doubt about were they dropped from a plane or a car and Laversuch proved it was a plane and GHQ were so relieved it was not a car that they congratulated him and said it was a model of deduction and information. It is rather interesting about reports and I did not know how really good ours were until later on I came to be reducing police reports and then I knew what hours of labour the Section had spared me. It really is quite extraordinary how police reports can disguise what facts you want to know, perhaps it is so simple to them they feel it would look bare without some decoration and can they and do they provide it, it is really quite extraordinary.

Accuracy is very interesting too. Anybody in a position of responsibility knows the importance of accuracy but then there are comparatively so few who have the responsibility of not being able to pass it on that the accuracy of anything does not trouble them the unresponsible ones who pass it on. We ofcourse were trained in accuracy but it is not training that makes it accurate it mostly is practice and practice is trial and error. In security work anything inaccurate makes such complications that you get to be accurate, that is first you get to be cautious and then you assess your information in varying degrees of reliability and you sift it out, then if it is an opinion you say it is and if it is more than an opinion and you know it then you say you know it but only what you do know of it. In this way mostly anything that begins suspicious usually ends not at all suspicious, it is disappointing but in security work it does save complications to be more accurate and not more suspicious.

It is very interesting this and in a way I think comforting, you do hear so often such fearful stories of flashing lights and signalling to the enemy and then always there is someone in any district who has German connections and you know for a fact if he is not a Nazi then he must be a Communist and what is the difference when nobody does anything about it. Ofcourse that really is what Security is for that nobody knows anything about it when something is done about it. It is very comforting to know that something is done about it. That is why I like being in an office in the middle of things because you do then know that something is done about it and it is very comforting, yes I think really on the whole it is quite comforting that perhaps not much may be done about it but something always is done about it. As I said Security is like the cockerel, it never can be sure that if it did not do anything about it there might then after all be something in it. Ofcourse it would be much more interesting and exciting if there was something in it but then after all that is what Security is for to prevent it being anything in it. Still there just is sometimes something in it and nobody knows it anything about it, mostly there is nothing in it it is more disappointing but much more comforting if nobody knows it and nothing is in it.

Ofcourse we were always hearing most fearful stories and the numbers of lights that were flashing at night in our little sector of northern France would I think have illuminated Blackpool at the height of its season. Mostly it was farmers bearing lanterns looking after sheep having lambs or seeing to it if their cows were having calves. Animals always do most things at the most inconvenient times and certainly lambs and calves are one of them the mayor of Givenchy once had a horse having a little horse at a most inconvenient time I was interviewing him about ringing the chapel bell as an air raid warning and the peasants when a bomb fell to be reporting it and not going near it till after it had gone off, the idea of delayed action bombs was quite new to them and new to us too and the mayor said it would go on being delayed until his horse had had a little horse and it took them three days it was fearfully inconvenient.

William France had a very bad farmer in his area a dangerous communist signalling to the enemy and he spent three dreary nights in a damp wood waiting for the hammer and sickle to be hoist with its own petard. Eventually he tracked the wicked creature down to a rather amicable gamekeeper who was vaguely socialist with nicely monarchist leanings. The principal if not the only dangerous thing was the gamekeeper's watch dog. It was and that was that.

There were various sorts of lights. There was a perfectly dreadful one I think it was in Hyland's area, everyone had a perfectly dreadful light sooner or later but this one was in Hyland's area and it took him several reports to get worked out the accuracy of it. I forget all the details but the chief ingredients were a French count his German mistress and a sinister visitor to their house of shame, anyway it was all very Oppenheim and Boris Kharloff and there was a marsh with a mist on it. Hyland turned on the accuracy and there emerged into the hard drab light of truth an eminently respectable French bachelor, a Polish maidservant and her Polish lover. While the bachelor dozed in his carpet slippers the little Greta would show a lighted candle from an upper chamber and by the time Boris Kharloff had traversed the mist and marsh she had slipped the well oiled bolt in the scullery door and met her lover there. Then up the stairs they crept, snuffed out the candle and well there they were, two Poles on a perch. After what we must suppose to have been a sufficient if not a very decent interval, the little Greta would relight the candle, descend the stairs, slip the well oiled scullery bolt, and send off Boris Kharloff into the murky morn. Unfortunately for them their performance was observed by a passing poacher, at least not all of it but quite enough to start a pretty story.

As Ashby said, it was a pleasing report but GHQ would never in the circumstances accept the accuracy of the French man's being a bachelor. Well anyway that was lights.

One of the things about accuracy besides its being the essential basis of reliable information is it necessarily determines the action to be taken. If action could be taken on suspicion only or on suspicious behaviour then probably half the adult population of the British Isles would be locked up tomorrow. Really anybody is suspicious if you think long enough about them in a suspicious way and even if you do not there are quite a number of people whose behaviour is sufficiently unlike anybody else's to make them suspicious to somebody. Anyway fortunately for them and for everyone taking action is a complicated process and it cannot often be performed without a most impressive accumulation of accuracy first. Ofcourse once the accumulation is there the action taken happens before you know it has begun and then it is just as complicated a process to get it undone as it has been to get it done.

The British way is to let the individual suspected do as much of the work as possible to get himself convicted. Before any action is taken against him they give him what they call enough rope to hang himself with and when he has given himself as much as he can they then step in and finish him off.

The French way is not the same way. If it was the same one would recognize it but one never could recognize it any of it as being quite the same as the British way. There were points of resemblance but what it was they resembled was what it was so difficult to see. Ofcourse to begin with there were all the regulations about identity and every one having papers of identity to establish the identity of each one, it was all very satisfactory if they had them but it was often very difficult to recognize that it was just as satisfactory to the French if they had them or had not. Mostly they had not.

Identity is one of the things it really is impossible to argue about, if you are you then your papers can not make you more you and if you are not you and your papers say you are you then how can you be you if you are not you, and that is identity. The French having had regulations about identity for a very long time know how impossible it is to argue about it and so they do argue about it thoroughly and often not because they are interested in identity which they know is a private matter but because talking and argument is a natural part of their speaking French. Really they know that anyone who relies on his papers to prove his identity and has all the papers that the regulations prescribe for having his identity really they have known for years he would not be a French one, so in this way any one who has his papers and in order is suspected and quite rightly arrested of not being a French one.

To prove all this we were often doing snap controls. Anyone now in England is knowing snap controls. It is when you are doing something in a hurry and they stop you and say who are you and you say who you are and they say what papers have you and if you have you show them and they then say this is the wrong one. You are in a great hurry and they say this is the wrong one, you know you are you you can not prove it you just do know it, they say it is the wrong one then you say you are in the home guard or ARP or whatever it is on the windscreen and the one with the bayonet stands with it fixed and the other one takes your papers to an officer and noone knows who is who but there are so many more that they have to do that they have to let you through. Really after all you know you are you and really after all you may be you and that is snap control. We were doing it often.

Now that in Britain we each of us are having our papers of identity our buff cards and our green cards we are beginning to realize the difficulties of identity, and it is a curious fact that anyone having a photograph of his identity is regularly saying it is not a good likeness and if it is not a good likeness a photograph is not good identity. In time we may come to be as knowledgeable as the French, that is we may keep on the regulations for the sake of uniformity and leave all the people in their natural obscurity. Any identity is a difficult thing and full of argument and the French do know it and are used to it and we are not. Ofcourse not.

Once William France was doing snap control with the French police, noone had any papers of identity but some had some papers and that in France is quite a good thing to have some papers and they were lightly fined or cautioned because the French police were on their dignity. Then one came along without any papers of identity or of anything else and the police were very nice to her and she walked through free. William France asked them why it was out of all the others she was not even admonished. The French police replied elle est institutrice et que voulez-vous, entre fonctionnaires. Well that is the French system and it is very beautifully French when you get to know it. Que voulez-vous entre fonctionnaires.

This naturally took us all a little time to realize.

The identity of Monsieur Soupe was quite a particular problem of identity. Houdret had gone to the town of Peronne and it was not very long before Houdret in his reports was mentioning Monsieur Soupe and who was he. Houdret was quite one of the most estimable members of our Section and still is. He has a veritable genius for getting to know everyone and getting on with everyone and in a French provincial town only a genius can get to know about everyone and still get on with them all. Anyway Houdret has this gift and I think it is because although he knows the gossip of every one he never says an unkind word of anyone. Monsieur Soupe immediately met him and asked him in to his café and bar. Monsieur Soupe was very interested in what Houdret was doing and what he had come for and Houdret became very interested in Monsieur Soupe being interested in him. Naturally. Then Houdret noticed how interested Monsieur Soupe was in the Air Force officers who came to his bar and then he was much more interested to learn that Monsieur Soupe was owning the land of the aerodrome.

In the office in Givenchy we were becoming interested in Monsieur Soupe and the weekly security report began having Soupe quite often in it. There was Soupe in morale, Soupe in rumours, and Soupe in British troops' relations with French civilians. Houdret then wrote a report how he learned that two years before the outbreak of war Monsieur Soupe had bought the grazing rights of a number of properties which were large flat and grassy and one of them was the aerodrome. Monsieur Soupe was often at the aerodrome gazing and grazing and he was often in his bar where the RAF boys went behind a curtain, and it was extraordinary how well informed Monsieur Soupe was about which planes were grazing and which were going and who was coming and little things like that. The weekly security report got to be having so much Soupe we really thought that GHQ might be interested but it was not. It said Soupe pish.

Then Houdret wrote a report that Monsieur Soupe had mentioned that besides his restaurant and bar he had a canteen also. After so much Soupe this was not very interesting and we wondered about the security report it had been rather a dull week but anyway we put the canteen in it, and instantly GHQ became highly excited. Could we definitely confirm that Monsieur Soupe had a canteen and was having a canteen and where and for how long it was very exciting. Houdret wrote back and said well actually no. Monsieur Soupe had said he had a canteen but actually he had not, it had been wishful thinking and GHQ was very angry and so were we and we asked Houdret to lay off Soupe and Houdret was well Houdret is never angry but he was chagrined.

He produced some very interesting facts about Monsieur Soupe's private life but we did not have a category for them, they were quite outside the category of morale so we could not put them into the security report so Houdret tried again. He sent a hair raising copy of a French police dossier and it was so hair raising it made a report of itself and we sent it in triplicate to GHQ and sat by the telephone all day. GHQ did not acknowledge it.

We were slightly bitter. We said to Houdret if there was anything in Peronne not Soupe would he please do it and he said there was not and furthermore there was Madame Soupe who was most intriguing she was sort of blonde and Bulgarian. We rang off.

Laversuch said he thought that Houdret might need a bit of psychoanalysing for a while to ease up the fixation. We said we thought he was a nice man but meant well.

Well anyway we got out all the reports there ever had been about Soupe there were about one hundred and fifty and we made him into a British Agent. This got him back into the security report in a sort of annexe to morale and GHQ never said a thing. But Houdret said well if he is a British Agent can he not be told that Houdret theoretically is on the same side of winning whatever it is at least for the duration if not a moment longer. We said we would do what we could. Ashby got on to GHQ and asked outright was Soupe British or not. GHQ said, well they said if he was British they had not been advised and if he was not they were still awaiting accurate information. We put away the one hundred and fifty reports and the security report had no Soupe in it for at least a week. We were fed up.

Then Houdret wrote that there was a canteen after all. Soupe had permission to start one, it had started yesterday and it was packed out, all the tea spoons had gone and everyone was furious and the RAF were livid with umbrage because the canteen naturally was for them and per ardua ad aspersions. And one of their aeroplanes had crashed into the canal and all the pylons and things had snapped off like matches, there was no light the canal was blocked and the mayor was absolutely furious there were no tea spoons the RAF were furious and everything was dreadful. Well this involved all our categories, there was the airplane accident was it sabotage and the pylons made the British troops' relations with French civilians, the tea spoons came under the intriguing one about thefts of petrol and clothing, the mayor was definitely morale and then ofcourse there was Soupe, all our categories were involved and the security report began to go to press.

Houdret then wrote another report, his reports ofcourse came by dispatch riders which made them more impressive than just posting them and ofcourse they were more secret but they took longer because sometimes it happened that one dispatch rider would arrive in the wrong order so the effect and the cause would be confused. We would wait to see if more dispatch riders arrived and Ashby would sit in his window looking on to the farm yard and then if no more came in we would work out the effect and the cause in the right order and Houdret said things were less dreadful but they were dreadful in a different way. The aeroplane had been rescued from the canal so the mayor was pacified and the drains were now more agreeable so that was all right. We said and the airplane was it sabotaged and Houdret said when he got there it had gone. We said what had gone where to, Houdret said every little bit had gone, there had been a saints day and everyone had been on holiday and he calculated that about three thousand inhabitants had now got a piece of the airplane in their pockets as a souvenir. Well really.

The security report had a little annexe to it that week about something about RAF property not coming within the province of Field Security or of any security. GHQ said nothing, well nothing to us and we went about our various ways with circumspection and righteousness.

Then GHQ suddenly telephoned and had we left out anything about anything dreadful happening. We said no but Ashby who has an immaculate memory for detail said yes we had left out tea spoons. GHQ said indeed, just indeed, and we then knew it had gone electrified at the other end of the line it was rather awful what was coming. We said yes Soupe, we were so sick of Soupe we said Soupe had said he had permission to open a canteen and he had opened a canteen and the tea spoons had gone from it like in any other canteen. GHQ said good gracious God, and the fastest car took them down to Peronne and Soupe well Soupe was not, he was not a British Agent.

Just fancy that.

6 *Givenchy 2*

So the weeks went by and Mondays regularly followed Sundays. We did our investigations in our little area and wrote our reports made contacts accumulated information and April now was May.

The information steadily accumulated and we passed it on. Each one had his lights and rumours to track down and his suspicious characters, his peculiar but harmless characters, his too talkative characters, his politically doubtful characters, and each one wanted watching and knowing assessing and reporting and it was necessary always in investigating them to make it certain that the amour propre of the French police was not impaired. If action should ever be necessary to be taken it was always most important to have their co-operation assured. It was not always easy but it always was necessary to have tact and patience and a flowing fund of conciliation and agreement. In our training they had taught us that if ever we were the means of what they called getting results we were to see that the credit for them was to be given to the French police. It would make them more disposed to help us if they could and yes it did. Still I must say that once or twice GHQ said they thought we were not to be despised. Only once or twice it was surprising. Well yes it was surprising because we were simply a very small means to an end, we simply accumulated information passed it on and what then became of it we never did know, in nine cases out of ten we did not know. We simply passed on information and they said please to remember we want the information accurate, we do not mind it seeming unimportant, you can not tell what is important but we can and what is accurate may be important. So we thought of our tea spoons and the information steadily accumulated.

The weeks went by and April now was May.

I did not much get outside being in the office all day but sleeping in the next village Manin I was walking back there in the evening and walking from it back to the office in the morning. In this way it was that spring was coming in the trees and hedges. The long straight avenue of tall straight trees to the chateau were budding silver, they were silver poplars very lovely in the early morning sun. There was a bank I passed beginning with blue bugloss it turned purple bugloss as purple as violets and then there were violets wild ones in creeping velvet patches. They were very lovely fresh with dewdrops and above them yellow celandines raising their heads above a coverlet of smooth green leaves. It was a pretty bank and a wood above it with white wood anemones in it. A little later when the grass was longer came elegant white bachelors buttons and rose pink campion and there were cowslips in the meadows and yellow buttercups and the silver slender poplars trembling in the breeze, it was a late but such a pretty spring.

Then one morning with the sun in a pale blue sky I saw in the woods round the chateau the shimmering breath of beeches. There is a quality about the early green of beeches that is like none other, it is the palest delicatest most virginal green, there is no blue nor yellow in it it is the youngest purest palest green and it is transparent. There was a mile long avenue of beeches stretching behind the chateau and I walked along it in the shimmering luminous palest youngest green. It is beautiful to be aware of early beeches with the sun in a pale blue sky.

I took a Sunday afternoon off and went into the country on my motor bicycle. Noone would say that this little area of northern France was beautiful country but there is in the country in any country so much of variety and growth and survival that the interest and the wonderment are always there. It is wonderful so much is fulfilled, it is not dead it rises again, struggles grows flowers seeds dies down is trampled on disappears, but it rises again in the country. In any country the wonderment is there and in any country the dead and trampled on rise up again, the spring comes back again and life will be fulfilled.

It was at this time I was observing the growth of French trees. French trees are interesting trees, it is not what they are but how they are planted is so interesting, French trees are more functional than British trees they belong to where they are and cannot be replaced by any other thing. It is a special quality they have French trees that they belong to the French countryside. Ofcourse they are used as everyone knows they are used in near buildings as architecture, even this quite inconspicuous but very dignified little chateau had its avenue of silver poplars and beautiful beeches and they could not be replaced by anything but trees. On the outside round the great stable courtyard they had a high clipped hedge of entwined chestnuts, it was a startling thing to a British mind to clip and train a flowering chestnut tree but to the French it was a functional purpose, it was arboreal architecture and very justified. And then they had two copper beeches the most beautiful copper beeches I have ever seen, they were given space and air and a perfect setting and they in their places were also justified.

Givenchy was just on the border line where the last world war had reached to, on one side was everything that had been, on the other side what was there was new and how you could tell it instantly the dividing line was by the trees. It was interesting and it was pleasing to see how the French must first of all before they built their houses first had planted their trees. On the roadways going to Arras the twenty year old trees were once again coming to begin there making avenues. I was going one day well beyond Lille to a little mining village and how desolate it was, how scarred and fearful it still was in the aftermath of the first world war, and you could see French families living now in the old and rusty Nissen huts lived in once by the fathers of the soldiers who were living in the newer Nissen huts of 1940 in adjoining fields. It was like the squalid tenements and houses were thinking it was not worth bothering to be fresh and clean again and no it was not worth bothering now but the French had planted their trees like they belonged to where they were, it was worth while bothering with their trees.

Givenchy was just on the border line of 1918 devastation and I once asked Madame of the farm what she remembered of the last world war. She said she had seen twenty Uhlans. The daughter-in-law who was hearing her telling me said yes Maman do tell us again what you saw in the last world war, and she said I saw twenty Uhlans. I saw them coming through the wood I was a young girl then and they were German Uhlans and I ran as fast as I could but I saw them coming through the wood. That was all. It was all that Madame could really remember of the last world war that there were twenty German Uhlans coming through a wood. I was very interested and I then asked the other elderly women in the village what they really could remember and they did not remember. One remembered it was not possible any more to go to market with her flowers and vegetables, eggs fruit cheese and honey she remembered it was awkward, but chiefly it was strange the change of having not a market. We could not meet our friends she said, c'était drôle it was strange. Another one, this was the one in the café made my supper in the evenings said she mostly remembered that everyone had gone, I said do you mean the village was evacuated, oh no she said the men had gone and it was left for us alone to do the work, we were too busy to be thinking about the war she said, the men had gone we had to do their work. That was the last, the first world war, the men had gone the women did their work.

I was having my afternoon off. The countryside was flat

where I was riding my motor cycle but by turning up a side track I came to a crease in the smoothness and I went down a steep hill into a screened valley. I came to a little hamlet lying in some woods and found a large meadow into which I wheeled the machine, turned off the engine, and lay down on the grass. It was completely peaceful and still.

It seemed impossible we were involved in war, nothing was happening, everything was still. There was nothing really to remember it by, it was like what the village women had told me about the last world war that they could not really remember it. They spoke of it in a curiously objective way, the war, like it had been an election or a fête. It was like a sort of period of time they were a part of but not affected by, like the summer or the winter or the harvest, the war the peace the spring the sowing the haymaking, it was like that. Let me see now, they would say, she had gone there in the war, or she had been there in the spring, or when it was war he had gone away and he came back afterwards when it was the time of harvest that would be after the time of war. It was not an interruption in their way of living the war the peace the harvest, it was an alteration in the continuation of their living. When they came to it they labelled it war or peace or harvest and when the phase was passed they labelled it differently. It could not be remembered as being really different it was not an interruption it was an alteration, really it was a continuation of their way of living.

And now it was happening again and nothing was really happening differently, it was a repetition of a certain phase of living which was labelled war, it was worrying and perplexing, so much had been so worrying and perplexing so many governments and politicians and political parties, there had been shooting and killing in Paris and now they were saying it was war. There had been so much trouble and struggle in France and now this trouble they said it was war, nothing really was happening differently, it was a repetition of what they were living, it was a phase of their living they were going through, the men were all going they labelled it war, they had been through it all so often before.

It was happening again but what were they doing differently.

The women all worked from dawn to dusk ploughing sowing hoeing milking cooking washing selling and buying but mostly ploughing and sowing as they had done before. They wrested a living from this cold flat land as though it were a battle with the sullen soil, and indeed it was. They had fought the same battle year after year generation after generation, never winning it outright, never assured of brilliant victory, for ever on guard against the elements' conspiracy. It was the sort of struggle they understood these tireless peasant women, it was their life and livelihood, their life had never been without it, their living was ever a struggle gaining one year losing the next, one could not be sure. Yet their life went on.

In this way I think it was they were thinking of the war, of this war, the last war, the 1870 war. It was part of the struggle of wresting a living, the women fought the elements' conspiracy and the men fought the Germans, generation after generation, it was part of the same long struggle, gaining one year losing the next, one could not be sure. I did feel somehow to these French peasant women that the Germans had become a part of the elements' conspiracy.

So the older ones were struggling in their working for a living, they were accepting it as their fathers had accepted it, that is willingly and proudly and on the whole contentedly, or if not contentedly then resignedly but on the whole quite happily. After all for these French peasant older ones it did not take them many grandfathers grandfathers to remember what their living had been before they had the right to live at all. In their peasant ownership it was a reminder to them that their struggling for a living was a struggle for themselves and that reminder gave them their contentment and their pride. But the younger ones, I think the younger ones were brooding more. They said, anyway there was a phrase most often being said il faut en finir, it must stop. There must be an end to it, they said. At first I thought it meant the Germans must be stopped, the German menace must be put an end to once and for all, then gradually I thought il faut en finir meant more what it said, it must stop, the eternal struggle must stop, the everlasting battling for a living must stop. Perhaps to begin with the young ones did not mean it so but I think the young ones did not have the philosophy nor the contentment nor the resignation and acceptance, nor the understanding of the reminder of their grandfathers grandfathers that the older ones had had. And then gradually I think that by saying il faut en finir it must stop they came to be intending that it should stop.

The younger ones brooded more, and then they were bored. At least the younger ones were in the village of Givenchy. When a nation is at war it is not good for it that the younger ones feel bored. The French were dreadfully bored.

I think it was at this time when April now was May that we were beginning to feel anxious in our minds. The cause of our anxiety was more than the Norwegian campaign and the shocking assurances of Mr. Chamberlain's junta of old men that all was better than could be revealed. One week we each of us were asked to send in a report about morale and we each of us said that morale was fair but would be improved by news of an allied victory. Then a little later, we were asked to do the same thing and this time I remember there was a difficulty about writing what we said in the weekly security report. We did not like to write what we knew was the truth, that morale was low and dropping lower.

It was curious this how none of us wished to believe what we knew to be true. We covered our misgivings by saying that anyway the relations between British troops and French civilians were always excellent. And they were. The British press and the usual government spokesmen had said they were so it was natural to us that we should doubt it but they really were, they always were excellent. I do not know about relations between the higher ranks but in the lower ones they were friendly and excellent. In this way we were able to assure ourselves that the French people's cordiality to the British troops signified some confidence in them, what we did not realize was their feeling of complete dependence on what British troops were there. But we were beginning to realize that the French people were feeling no confidence in themselves nor in the issue. They were bored they were anxious they were unreliable.

We were saying now that if the Germans after all did not

attack this spring and summer the French would collapse in the autumn without striking a blow. They were slowly but quite certainly disintegrating. I remember very clearly in the office we were saying that the French would collapse without striking a blow, the reports coming in from our area said as much. The women wanted their men back and particularly they wanted to attend to the harvest. The men in the forces had been trained to defend, they had not been trained to attack, there was no attack which they could defend, they were earning no money and they were bored. But there was more than all this, they had no will to win, they did not think they could win, they knew they would not win. We heard so often the same French story that France poor France had nothing the Germans had everything and the British how could they help poor France they had a navy but how could they help poor France. I said once to the daughter-in-law of Madame and perhaps I was tired and a little angry I said but the French have they not got a big strong army, and she began to cry a little. They will all be killed she said, the Germans have everything and France poor France has her frontiers to defend, how can she do it when the British have no army they have a navy but what use is that to France with her frontiers to defend. I said and the Air Force have we not an Air Force. Ah yes she said, the British say they have an air force but the Germans they have everything and France poor France has nothing. It was like a refrain. It was depressing and ungovernable.

We were all of us wondering a good deal about this, it was worrying. It was not surprising, after all we most of us had lived in France for some time and on the Continent it was not surprising that the French were feeling like this. It was a part of everything that had been happening to them for a quarter of a century and it was a part of everything had been happening to democracy for some time longer, and it was a part of nationality and loyalty patriotism a kingdom a republic and party strife and unemployment and bankruptcy, everything. When they say how disgraceful it is that the French have fallen and they will never rise again how can it be disgraceful that they have been through everything and suffered so much, it was the end of a chain of chronic circumstances. What they were suffering in their democracy and helpless inertia was the difference between the French and British peoples was very nearly hardly anything, it simply was the French had had a little more of democracy and politics than we had had and they simply could not stand them any more, they could not stand anything any more. We were not very far behind them and still and afterwards how much are we going to be behind them.

The French have had so many things happen to them that they can take disaster as a thing they are used to, that is as an interruption. The French are not a consecutive people like the British in their institutions they are interrupted, their monarchies are interrupted their republics are interrupted their policies their parliaments and their politics are interrupted. I think it is important to understand this that the French in their institutions are often interrupted and they themselves are not. The French are individualists what is inside each one is kept quite private as a hard unchanging core, and it really is because they have this inside core they do not mind their institutions being interrupted. What the French have private inside each one Miss Gertrude Stein says very well she says with any people but the French you would imagine that this well not secrecy but not telling would have something a little unpleasant about it but with the French it is a serious comedy that makes them that more attractive. Their lives are their own it is not a secret but one does not tell it. And she says and beside that Frenchmen do not really think they have anything to do with anything that governs, they live their own life and they fight for that country and beside that they have no responsibility. Their life is secret that is it belongs to themselves and up till now that is what has made French elegance and French style, it is a funny story.

In our dealings with the French and naturally that was what we in France were there for to be dealing with them in our speaking and translating French, it was this not telling us what they were feeling made it sometimes so troubling. It is difficult to explain this thing, it is not reticence it is not a withdrawal it is not caution or shyness and certainly not resentment, it just is something one does not tell. And so it was we could not help them and noone could not really help them. We were it was our duty to help strengthen their morale restrict rumours stop panics, we were there to do what we could. But we could not, always we came up against this hard not secret but incommunicable core, this fear this foreboding this boredom this France poor France, this il faut en finir.

Ofcourse it was not that everyone went about with long and wretched faces. The peasants as I have said the peasants we were among were far too busy in their ordinary living to have much time for unhappy speculation, and when disaster came its shock and swiftness swept away all thought but that of the urgent peril of the individual instant. But in these early days of May we were feeling the undercurrent of uneasiness spreading like a rampant binding weed. Noone seemed really happy in France, they seemed obsessed with the idea of disaster. There again they did not say it, they simply did not tell it. They seemed unhappy and anxious and they all seemed tired, so dreadfully tired. I came to see then the importance of their institutions being interruptions, they were experiments. That is one of the characteristics of republics that they are made and counted and stopped and begun again and counted again. In England it is a kingdom is consecutive it is not counted and in England even the government once it becomes the government is like any other government it is consecutive and much the same but in France it is not, a government is a political party and which ever gets in is different and quite different, it is interrupted and is counted and is thrown out and a different one gets in and France being not a kingdom is a republic is counted the first the second and the third and each is different and is a different experiment. The French were feeling that their third republic was an experiment and it was time it was interrupted. It has been interrupted.

So in France a republic and England a kingdom they are different but being a democracy they are the same, not quite the same but as much is enough. It was this their democracy that made the difference between the French and the British very nearly hardly any. Democracy has always worried me terribly and when you will remember when the war first started how they tried to justify its moral basis by going right through everything. You will remember first how it was saving international law and all those wretched little lamps of Europe going out, then it was saving the Germans from themselves, then they tried christianity and then they tried democracy. When I joined up I began asking everybody if they were saving democracy and they did not say yes, a great many of them said on the contrary they were fighting to finish it. I do think this is true that a great many are still against saving democracy and certainly if they have a victory and are given back their democracy as they were having it then certainly they will fight another war and if absolutely necessary even a civil war to finish it. The French had suffered from democracy even more than the British had, and is it not true they are beginning now having their civil war, economically financially and politically and spiritually they had suffered even more and really they could not bear it any more. They have been waiting for an interruption. There had been shooting and fighting in Paris, it was the starting of the interruption. They kept on asking is it civil war, they all expected civil war, they did not want it they just waited for it to begin. And yes it did begin and in France they did not know it had begun. It had begun in Spain that they could recognize but when it began in France they did not recognize it until too late. They were waiting for it to begin and it had already begun, they did not know it, it was done.

One of the curious things about democracy is the people have so little to do with it. They wait for something to happen and when a decision is made they are told it is their decision but really it is not, all the important decisions have been made before they are told and all the lesser decisions they are advised upon and they say yes or no and that is their decision. Sometimes it is that they make a decision, the people make a decision and it is surprising how upsetting it then is, it is so upsetting that the machinery of democracy has to be stopped to be adjusted. This only happens once in five or seven years and it is coming to be felt that even that is too often but it is not, the machinery of democracy goes on much the same whether the people make a decision or do not, they call it an adjustment but the wheels go running round and if they make a decision it is much the same as if they do not, really the same people decide what is important and the wheels run round. In the French democracy the people had given up trying to make a decision, the political parties did all the deciding and the people just stood or sat where they were reading the papers and the posters and hearing the political parties and why make any decision. They were waiting for something to happen, they did not know what would happen but they did know that something would happen. I have said in Le Havre I had this feeling that something would happen they did not tell it and they did not know what, but it was going to be bad. They made no decision they waited and it was bad. Anybody in France was feeling this thing it was going to be bad it was innate and ungovernable.

If you do not mind I will quote again Miss Gertrude Stein writing about the French democracy she says. When French people read political posters they do not converse about it or about anything. They have been through so many things and they know that it makes trouble for them that naturally when they read them they just silently read them. It is like the women in Bilignin the farmers wives the first thing they asked me when we came down this summer it was well before the Spanish revolution they asked me is there going to be a civil war oh dear is there going to be civil war, that is one of the curious things about a European democracy they do not feel that they have any more to do or say about what is going to happen than when it was a kingdom that is the reason to our surprise the return of the empire or the kingdom is not at all a surprising thing, after all they do not know who decides these things all they know is that there is a decision.

That is true for the French nation and it is important and it is true and exceedingly important for us the British nation. Afterwards it will be more important after all we are fighting now for our existence but afterwards we are fighting not for a reversion to democracy but for a renewal of democracy and who decides these things is more important much more important than that there has been a decision, after all what is our existence going to be for. We shall see and yes we will see.

In this atmosphere of tension, no tension is too strong a word but in this despondent expectancy we were waiting for a decision to be taken. What would be the outcome of this silent civil war of the fighting treacherous political parties while the masses looked on despondent discontented and almost disinterested. In these early days of May the French had imprisoned fifty of their members of Parliament and had sent at least three thousand agitators into concentration camps. Yet the Communists were quite undaunted and were working hard amongst the troops and in the factories. They reinforced the general cry il faut en finir.

Scarcely distinguishable from them in so far as the war effort was concerned were the Isolationists who were busy and vociferous in the parliamentary lobbies, insisting that the position was insoluble, the strategical position was insoluble, insisting upon a European settlement. They eagerly swallowed and heartily endorsed the German propaganda that the British army was too small to be effective and that France had been dragged into the war by Great Britain over Poland. They demanded what they called an honourable peace before the British had forced France to fight, and to fight they said she did not want to do. The alternative was a continuation of indefinite stalemate, the situation was insoluble, a settlement must be made, they said.

This attitude was shared by probably a majority of French people, perhaps especially by the women. The food restrictions, the trials of evacuation, neglected farms, failing businesses, the general inconvenience, and the feeling of frustration converged and found expression in their constant cry, il faut en finir. They saw their men folk herded and embedded in the Maginot Line and their men folk writing home expressed their growing boredom. Was it not inevitable that a feeling of futility should materialize.

Opposed to the agitators, the isolatonists, the confused masses and the great traitors were the Activists, struggling to infuse some order into the general chaos, trying under Reynaud to prosecute the war. It was a hopeless task. The Reynaud government was expected to fall at any time any week, almost from hour to hour. This was France in May 1940. Not a shot had been fired, not a bomb had been dropped. She was on the verge of collapsing and sueing for peace.

Then the Germans struck her. They attacked at Sedan. It was like a douche of ice cold water. France staggered. Could she collect her shattered wits in time.

In our office at Givenchy we had a large scale map on the wall. We looked at Sedan. We were not greatly worried. We were not greatly worried because we knew that if and when the Germans attacked they would attack at Sedan. Everyone knew that, Jacques the French interpreter at the chateau knew it, it was quite common talk. At Sedan the Maginot line proper ended there. Thence, curving north to meet the Belgian frontier, a secondary line had been constructed and this in turn had ended and given place to a line of fortifications along the Belgian frontier which the BEF had been constructing all the winter. At Sedan then there was this gap in the Maginot line, like a hinge, but there was a compensation in the hilly wooded terrain which German tanks, pushing through the gap, would find it difficult to negotiate. It was a terrain ideal for tank traps and ambushes.

The German armoured divisions burst through the gap. There was so little resistance there must be a trap. We watched them coming onwards on our map.

Jacques the interpreter came in every evening to our office to hear the wireless news from London. He began to be worried. We still were not, there must be a trap we said, it was part of a plan. Jacques grew more worried and then we began being worried. Jacques said and he would be pacing up and down twisting his hands and he said it so often Gamelin Gamelin I do not trust him on n'a pas de confiance, on n'a point de confiance. We were disturbed in our feelings.

Then one morning early Houdret telephoned from Peronne. French troops are marching through the town he said. All last night and still this morning French troops are marching through in large numbers. We asked which way. Southwards and eastwards he said. Good we said have they got tanks. No he said. Oh we said, oh lord.

Laversuch rang up Major Watson at HQ about the French troops marching southwards through Peronne to meet the Germans coming northwards from Sedan. Major Watson said could we trace the source of the rumour and send in a report. Laversuch rang off, furious.

Later on we were told that this item of news had been of some interest to HQ. It was the first authentic information they had received from the south. I dare say it was not the first but that is what we were told.

We tried the wireless all day it was jammed. I think it was the French jammed it because we could not get even German stations, we could not get any stations.

The next morning Houdret rang up very early. He said the French troops were coming back again. We said what. He said yes they are pouring through Peronne in confusion and disorder, they say their officers have deserted them. We said good God you come back here at once.

We looked at the map. We realized what had happened. There had been no trap, there had been just a gap. We could hardly believe it. We said it must be treason. We were probably wrong. We heard that in that vital gap the French command had placed only second rate troops. They had broken and fled, reinforcements were rushed up, also second rate, and Houdret was seeing them now fleeing back in disorder. It had been estimated that they would kill 250,000 Germans before leaving their positions. The author of the Diary of a Staff Officer was present at the allied generals' conference held after the Germans had taken Sedan and he says: 'The conference was a tragic affair. Most of the French officers were in tears, some quite openly sobbing at having to admit the shame they felt in acknowledging the appalling fact that the French had walked out of their fortified positions without any attempt at genuine resistance.'

We told Houdret to leave Peronne at once. We then told everyone to report back to the office and they did. Hyland from

Albert, Barnes from St.Pol, Crew and Norris from Bienvillers and Beaumetz and Morris from Frévent. Wright Pound and France were close at hand in Manin. Lovegrove had left us for Scandinavia. Laversuch and Parham the driver slept in the office to be near the telephone. When Laversuch was called out I took his place.

The French had stopped saying il faut en finir. Now they were saying with grave sad faces ça commence. Ça commence. I think they felt it was the beginning of the end.

Did we, we did not. We were very cheerful, often hilarious. The weather was continually dry and sunny, there was a feeling of adventure in the air, and we were very healthy and very happy. We had a sense that the long period of waiting and suspense had ended, now things were going to happen. What these were we did not know and we were too busy to wonder. I think it is true that none of us at any time consciously envisaged the catastrophe ahead and none of us thought ever in terms of disaster. It is not possible when everything is happening to think in terms of catastrophe and disaster. It just is not possible. We were soon to know.

Our time at Givenchy was drawing to a close. We were exceedingly busy. To begin with the troops in our neighbourhood were all moving forward and new ones were moving up and taking their places. We had to be watchful. The outgoing troops had a habit of leaving various things behind. Norris brought in a bundle of papers found in fragments in a waste paper basket. We pieced them together with glue on cardboard. The Germans would have been highly interested had they found them. The regiment was warned to be more careful. And once Houdret found some papers in the chimney of a stove and the stove had not been lighted. He sorted them out and took action. The password was Norway. He got on his motor cycle and pursued the troops. He caught them up after darkness. Who goes there they said. Norway he said and passed on. Who goes there some more of them said. Norway he said and rode right on. He reached the chateau marked on the unburnt papers. A sentry barred his way, Norway said Houdret, okay said the sentry, and Houdret walked into the hall. It was midnight and divisional headquarters. Good evening gentlemen he said. Who the devil are you they said. Norway he said. Oh they said. Houdret just quietly explained. They were extraordinarily kind and polite. The adjutant personally saw he was made comfortable for the night. And this indeed was a generous gesture considering how personally uncomfortable the adjutant was going to be that morning. Houdret left before the trouble started. I expect they lighted every stove they ever came across for ever after.

Anyway the troops were moving on and new ones were coming. We made contact with them. Movement was general. Dumps were moving, ammunition petrol food cars lorries guns ordnance. We scouted around on our motor cycles, reported their positions and marked them on our large scale map. It was necessary to make sure they were properly guarded and adequately concealed and their position not indicated by road signs or other signs. Were they, in a word, secure.

Testing the security of an ammunition dump was an anxious business. We could rely on the ammunition remaining reasonably controlled but what the sentries would do was beyond our conjecture. On the whole I think they were as terrified of us as we were of them, they could not have been more so.

We were often arrested. Usually they were quite nice about it but sometimes they were not. One naughty old colonel said we ought to be shot. Haven't you bloody well got anything better to do than bloody well go nosing around. We said we bloody well had not. He was furious. The boys in the guard room were delighted.

Once one of us got arrested and they rang up the office and we said which one, they said he says he is Norris. We said well why not. They said he is very suspicious we do not like the looks of him and he has a moustache. We said well then that is not Norris and rang off. Hours later they rang up again, they said we can not shake him he swears he is Norris and he has a moustache. We said are you sure. They said, hold on. We heard something going on at the other end of the line and they came back. They said it won't come off nohow. I think it was Pound then said if you are talking about Norris he started a moustache last week. We told them that. Well anyway Norris was very sensible about it and we gave him some stuff to put on and it got better and now he is an officer they cannot do such things with impunity good heavens no.

Then the parachutists came, tens dozens scores twos and threes and hundreds of parachutists. They were a fearful nuisance. They meant hours of work. It would have made it so much easier if they had existed but existence was the one thing they lacked. Practically anything was a parachutist. Anything visible was a parachutist like the anti-aircraft puffs of smoke and the trails of aircraft in the sky, and then birds and things in the air and then haystacks and gypsies priests nuns and geese in a meadow and finally once two young lovers with a half day off in a wood. Four hundred troops surrounded the wood and four generals and they said, whatever one does say to parachutists come clean or something, and they did not. They were two French lovers in a wood and they did not come clean at all. So the four hundred troops fixed bayonets and marched in to the wood and the four generals and well there they were. The FSP did all the translating of what each side said to the other, it took a very long time but almost it was worth it. Major Watson said do a report on relations between British troops and French civilians, we used our discretion and that was parachutists.

Then there were leaflets. Noone liked leaflets much more than parachutists but at least they were there. They did exist and in looking for something existence is useful. We thought so the French did not, the French were not interested. They wanted to get in the harvest and finish the war and the leaflets did not tell them how to do either, the leaflets mostly told them what a good kind man Adolf Hitler was and the French were not interested but perhaps they are now. In one of the leaflet raids, the searching began in the early hours of daylight to pick them all up before they could be seen and read, we met an old peasant and we asked him what he thought of leaflets and his reply was interesting. He said the thing he mostly thought about was how British ever stood a man like Mr. Chamberlain and how much more would they stand of him.

So our days in Givenchy were coming to an end. There was a sense of movement and parachutists and leaflets, among the French sense of foreboding, among ourselves a sense of excitement and of something going to happen.

One day we went to the chateau for our midday meal and saw the secret installation being packed away in a closed in van. Every one was going, HQ were moving out. Soon there would be nothing but the long straight avenue of tall straight trees and the copper beeches standing in their finest summer glory.

Everyone was going that is the British not the French, the men were all going and the women were staying. They ploughed the fields and sowed the grain, milked the cows fed the horses carried the water and did the cooking and the cleaning and the washing. Yes Madame was the one who did everything a grand old peasant woman not old in years but old in her wisdom and in her strength as old as France is old.

They labelled it war or peace or harvest and when the phase was passed they labelled it differently. It was a phase of their living they were going through, they labelled it war, they had been through it all so often before. Yet their life went on.

It was a late but such a pretty spring, there were cowslips in the meadows yellow buttercups and rose pink campion. And the silver slender poplars whispered gently in the breeze. Madame had heard them so often before. She knew she would hear them again.

Givenchy-le-Noble is a very small village not a pretty one. Quite flat it is and a little hill comes down each side of it and into it a road runs through it there is a second one bisecting it in the middle of the village and twenty small houses that is all.

It had been our home and kind to us. We had rested there.

PART THREE: THE RETURNING

7 *Avesnes*

It happened at six in the morning.

Before it happened things had been happening that is to say they had been gradually happening and German planes had come over our way. They would come over by day and then they would go away. We said they were British planes or French planes to comfort the French and encourage them but they said they were German planes because France had nothing the Germans had everything and so they were. Then there were more and gradually more of them.

One day they bombed Arras rather badly and some of it was burnt. Ofcourse in those days bombing was still as a shocking surprise and just a little of it was enough. Later on when bombing became a daily occurrence areas thrice the size of Arras were, well they sustained considerable damage to household property and the casualties were either not numerous in proportion to the scale of the attack or they had a supplementary bulletin to themselves that the casualties were then feared to be higher than it was at first thought possible for casualties to be. It is curious and awful how bombing has developed from what it was to what it is, awful because it is accepted and has to be accepted as a part of our living and curious that it is acceptable. After all it is curious hardly anyone believes the official bulletins of bombing, noone really believes our bombers hit everything of importance the German bombers miss everything of importance, all the ordinary people know too much of bombing now to believe the official bulletins of what they say the bombers do and so it is the British people and the German people have the bombing and know it and the official people have their bulletins and know them. Neither side believes the other naturally not but that they do not believe their own side is curious.

Well anyway but before that when Arras was bombed just a little was enough. Lord Hawhaw said they would bomb the station and they did. Then he said they would bomb the cathedral and they did. Actually they did not but everyone believed they did so it was as good as doing it. The night I am coming to when it happened at six in the morning they bombed Arras again and I was at Manin sleeping there and I saw some of it through a window. Then they came over Manin and bombed some gun emplacements. It was disturbing but not alarming.

And then almost immediately there was Parham in the room. He said come quick. I came.

Major Watson had telephoned. He said pack everything destroy everything report to Avesnes in five minutes. That was at six.

The Germans had taken Peronne.

We destroyed everything and said goodbye to everyone and destroyed everything again. We took everything out of the office into the farm yard, poured petrol on the heap and burnt it. Maps plans reports files stationery pay rolls telephone numbers official documents the card index Army Council Instructions and the Kings Regulations, everything. Then we went on our motor bikes in a roaring line to Avesnes.

Nothing happened at Avesnes for about two hours. We took everything off our bikes and put it on them again compressed and secure. We were parked up a lane. A huge French gun was in a field. Its crew were indescribably dirty and about forty of them.

Someone in GHQ said we were to go in pairs about the town to study morale. France and I went off and had a chat with some women and were immediately reported by them to a CMP who immediately arrested us. Then we had lunch. The CMP was tired but charming.

Avesnes was very excited in a way but it was suppressed. It was like an English town on market day with a Conservative Fête in the afternoon. Everyone knew what would happen and they were quite as excited as if they did not. There were a great many people had come in from the surrounding districts and then a great many more began coming through and then suddenly everywhere was full of them and it began.

The refugees had started.

We were taken off morale and put on traffic control. I was at the cross roads at the foot of the town by the chateau, the chateau where we had sent in our security reports in the weeks gone by. There was one thing to do with the refugees, keep them moving and keep them moving straight on. On and on, on on and on.

This was the first day it was all cars, Belgian cars and French cars and some Dutch cars but mostly French and Belgian cars. I forget how many it was that passed in an hour but there was never a break in between. They came on and on, on on and on.

There were hundreds of cars, thousands of refugees. They all looked much the same and one car looked much the same as the next one coming after. On the top there were always the mattresses laid flat on the roof and on them lay blankets pillows eiderdowns rugs and these were securely corded and then usually a bicycle and a child's scooter and sometimes a pram securely corded on top of them. It was hot and dry and it was all right, later on it was cold and wet and then it was not so all right. Inside the cars there was everything the family had and all the women inside all wore little round hats with little veils on them. The children usually there were two or three children they were usually asleep. There were never any pet animals and the windows were tight shut though it was hot but they were closed. Perhaps it is not kind to say they all looked very bourgeois but they did, they were plump scented and stuffy.

So the cars and refugees passed on and on and that was the first day.

These first ones did get through to Paris. The later ones did not. The Germans cut up from Sedan and Peronne through Albert Amiens and up to the coast cut all communications so the refugees streaming westwards were caught and sent back eastwards. But still thousands more were streaming westwards met these streaming back eastward ones, so everyone was caught and everywhere was blocked.

The next day again we did traffic control and again at Avesnes and for two days more. The second day the cars were different they were slower and shabbier and the second day began the bicycles. There is one thing only to say about the bicycles, they were ridden all of them hundreds I should say thousands of them were all ridden by young men and the Belgian ones had scarlet blankets. We did ask them where they were going and what they were doing. Some of them laughed and went on. Others said they had orders to report to the military authorities at Albert to be formed there in to regiments and given uniforms and arms. This was a genuine idea and I did hear afterwards they were all caught there and made prisoners before even they had reported to the military authorities. Ofcourse by the time they reached Albert it had been German for some days.

The next day the third day the refugees were still some bicycles but mostly now they were peasants walking and some in incredibly frail looking creaking buses and some in carts drawn by big Flemish broad horses. These horses were the most intelligent looking of those passing for they had a sense of direction. We asked we often asked these people where they were going and they none of them knew where to. Not one of them knew where to they followed their horses.

We did traffic control from about 8 in the morning till between 9 and 10 at night. It was dark then and the stream then ceased. In Avesnes everyone was occupied that is in the cafés and restaurants they were occupied, and in a small French town nothing much else matters and they were doing a roaring trade. Then on the third day we went in and everything had stopped. Everyone was sitting down and crying. We were concerned.

In a way our job besides traffic control was to keep up morale and then with everyone just sitting down and crying made it difficult. We found out why it was. Early that morning some French troops had passed through. They had come up from Peronne. They had no arms and were saying that the struggle was hopeless. They said that the Germans were invincible.

I remember so well our consternation. It was imperative to prevent a panic. The streams of refugees were demoralizing enough but at least they kept the inhabitants occupied in attending to their needs. But seeing French soldiers just scattered and adrift was another matter. We found the people sitting in their shops and cafés crying and hopeless, men as well as women. We harangued. We argued exhorted bullied coaxed joked cheered them up. They revived a little. We got the soldiers on to a lorry and sent them away.

Their story was grim all the same. They were some of the soldiers who had fled from Sedan. They had watched from their fortified posts the German hordes coming on. First a line of tanks advanced. They were blown to pieces by the French guns. After the tanks marched rows of soldiers marching shoulder to shoulder. They were mown down by machine gun fire. Behind them came another line of tanks, then rows of soldiers, then tanks, then soldiers. A French poilu described the scene to me. The Germans were hidden in a wood he said. An officer blew a whistle and hundreds of them fell in, shoulder to shoulder, in lines on the edge of the wood. The whistle blew again, they marched, following the tanks before them. Behind them more tanks followed them on. The officer blew his whistle again, hundreds more men fell in, the whistle blew, they started marching, another batch shoulder to shoulder, marching on in solid rows between the lines of tanks. They could not escape, the Frenchman said. Those who escaped the bullets were caught by their own tanks tolling on behind, the dead the dying and the wounded were crushed to death by wave after wave of tanks. And the soldiers behind, shoulder to shoulder, trampled the shattered limbs and bodies of their fallen friends.

And they were singing, he said. His voice dropped into itself as he saw again the spectacle of horror. They were singing Nazi war songs, marching shoulder to shoulder, their eyes fixed, staring ahead, trampling through the blood and flesh of their own people, not hearing their screams nor caring for their fate. They are not human, he said, his voice with a shudder in it. They do not belong to the human race. No man out of woman can do such things. He can not do it. He can not do it.

The little poilu, dirty dishevelled unshaven, recoiled with his body. He made a gesture with his arm, not of fear or cowardice but of withdrawing from something unspeakably unclean. We cannot fight, he muttered, we cannot fight such monsters.

That morning M. Reynaud broadcast to the French people. France, he said, was in danger, in mortal danger. Her sons and daughters must keep calm. France had been in peril before, she had been invaded, plundered, devastated, but she had survived. Her sons and daughters must not fail her now. They must not falter, they must come to her aid. France was in mortal peril. She needed the strength and courage of her children.

Yes her children, helpless bewildered deserted and betrayed. They had not honoured their fathers' sacrifice nor their days in the land of France their mother.

And now there was no bread. The refugees had eaten all the bread and noone had thought of making any more. There was no wine and no beer no milk no butter no cheese and no bread. There were some eggs.

That afternoon we went round every house in the town. If there were refugees staying in it they had to go. It was necessary to keep the town cleared of anyone extra in case of action. We put up a notice at the incoming end saying no refugees could stop in the town, they must go on and keep on going on. It was a job that took time and patience perseverance and politeness. Of Belgian refugees there were none. The French hated them like poison, they would not have them in their houses. But French families there were, whole families of them and each family had a history of woe. We had to listen to their stories, the interminable details of their private lives and all the reasons why they should be excepted from the order to go. Anyway after much patience politeness and perseverance they did go. In the evening we found they had just moved into the neighbouring barns on the farms and then I must say there was less oh much less patience and politeness all round.

On the fourth day the refugees were considerably less, after all we had seen several tens of thousands of them and then at last there were left just the stragglers. These were old men and old women just walking with bundles and children or just walking and pushing small carts with bundles and children in them. They did not know any more than anyone else where they were walking to but so long as someone told them to keep on walking they kept on walking. One of the last things I remember about the refugees in Avesnes was the last night there at about nine. Right down the main street came a great noise, it was a steam roller over the cobbles. Attached to the steam roller were two large open waggons and in them each were perhaps thirty women and children and old men and bundles and odd bits of things, and in the end one two small dogs and attached to the end waggon were two cows walking. The steam roller came down the street with its procession at three slow deafening miles and hour and it went on and on, I was at the cross roads, and it went on and on in to the night, on and on, on on and on. As one of the wheels slowly turned it made a shrill squeak. Every time it turned it made a squeak. For four days and nights from Belgium into France and across northern France at three miles an hour in an open waggon under the black smoke of the smoking chimney in a constant unchangeable shattering noise, this is how these families had lived. Why did they live. Did they live. Why should they live. Where could they live. And at regularly punctual intervals the wheel turned round and answered them, squeak. Squeak squeak. Squeak squeak squeak. I heard it fading into the unchartered night.

The next day we left Avesnes taking the big north road to St.Pol and beyond it to Béthune. Everywhere was refugees. Hundreds thousands and hundreds of thousands of refugees. Every road we went on there were refugees, helpless, motionless, listless, foodless. They had blocked themselves. They could not go on they could not go back. They were just there, just where they were.

I remember wondering so often about them why it was I could not feel some pity. I could not and I did not. I wondered about it a lot. There was something puzzling about these refugees, it was something more puzzling than not having pity because I was not rejecting pity I simply was not having any.

After a while I think I began to know the reason why. It was simple. Everything had happened to them before. Everything that was happening to them now had happened to them before and then gradually I came to see that refugeeing is a habit. A habit is what you are used to and you can not feel pity for what you are used to. I came quite clearly to see then that all these people had the habit of refugeeing in their blood and ancestry and that is what stopped them from being pitiful. It was simple. The children's fathers and mothers were now being what their fathers and mothers had been, and what their fathers and mothers had been was just what refugees have been.

The author of My First War says 'I suddenly realized the desperate precariousness of a refugee's life. Once they've left home – with their bicycles and bedding and bird-cages – they're venturing into the unknown. And if they lose a wife or a child they have no means of ever finding them again. The impulse of fear must be very powerful. It is significant that no one ever flees towards Germany.'

But it is not really significant and it is not fear it is habit and instinct. None of these refugees was frightened, they were tired and hungry worried bewildered and blocked but they were not frightened they were simply doing blindly what they all were doing and what their ancestors had been doing was fleeing from east to west and that is an instinct fleeing east to west.

War is an instinct and anything is more likely to be instinctive in war than anything else and refugeeing certainly is an instinct. Years ago that is centuries ago it became expedient to flee before the enemy for the enemy was always characterized and still is as being more armed ruthless and brutal than anyone else. But as the enemy was really not more armed ruthless and brutal than the other armed forces were then the civilian population quite naturally and very wisely quitted the scene of operations until the fighting forces had fought it out. When the enemy had won, and in early Britain this practically always happened that the enemy had won the civilian population came back again and intermarried and settled down until someone else became the enemy. The British population always fled from east to west like all the other European peoples. After the Italians had conquered us ofcourse they were called Romans then so we did not mind it so much, the British population began to stop fleeing from east to west but on the Continent the habit still persisted and people still ran about from east to west and then gradually whenever a war started it became the thing to do. When the French became the enemy of Europe it is to be noted that the population could not flee east to west but they did not either flee from west to east because they had not the habit nor the instinct to do so and what is there to flee to east when the English became the enemy the Americans did not flee to Siberia they fled to America and everyone knows they went west. In more recent times war has been much more like centuries ago because the enemy, which was characterized as German and still is, was characterized as being more armed ruthless and brutal. So once more it has been expedient to flee before the enemy from east to west and in that way the children's fathers and mothers are now being just what their fathers and mothers had been and what their fathers and mothers had been was just what refugees have been. It is a habit and instinctive.

The refugees went from east to west and we went from south to north and either way was long and hot and laboriously slow.

Before leaving Avesnes there was one other thing I ought to mention, it was the last thing we ever did there. We were all rather tired it was rather late and someone had been sent to find bread and he said yes there was some in the village. We arranged to go in shifts to have a meal there. I was in the last shift about 9-30 with Laversuch and I think it was Parham. We had just got there and were sitting down when a dispatch rider came in and said come on back quick to Avesnes. We had some bread and eggs and rushed back. There was a great commotion and excitement and GHQ and every one was there. It was parachutists. We groaned but this time they promised us genuine ones so we were mollified.

We all split up into parties on our motor bikes and GHQ led the way. It was like an armoured pheasant drive. My job was to patrol the town absolutely and take no chances. It was pitch black. I had a torch a revolver and a packet of chocolate. The two roads into the town were blocked and guarded. Where they came out of the town one was blocked and guarded and the other road past HQ in the chateau had a machine gun post.

Nothing much happened, except ofcourse in the dark where ever you went you were challenged by sentries and they wanted cautious handling. Soon after midnight shots rang out and a bullet whistled over head and there were lights in a field. It was one of the road posts thinking they were seeing some thing moving. But they were not, they were only thinking.

Then it was moonlight which was more comforting. At two oclock I was by the chateau and suddenly revolver shots went off very near me and then there were troops in a wood. It was an anxious moment who were they. The adjutant saw something standing there and it moved and he challenged it. It did not answer. He gave it the works and the troops closed in. It still did not answer. They found it standing there and as it was, it was a tallish white post when the moon shone the trees moved and that threw shadows on it and well naturally why answer. I must say the post was remarkably unscathed.

After that we had some rather hot tea.

There was still no news of the mechanized hunting party. At about five it was daylight, broad daylight and I then lay down in it by the side of the road. At six I woke up and there the party was.

It had been an interesting excursion and briefly it was this. When they had got to where the parachutists ought to have been they stopped and GHQ had a consultation on the spot. The first thing was to dismount all the guns off the lorries and they did and they then discovered that the ammunition though very good and plentiful was not the sort of ammunition that these guns should have. So the general asked for a torch to see for himself and there were no torches either. Someone who proffered matches was promptly put out. They then said all right all right let byegones be byegones until we get back and then by god by god let us look at the maps they said. So they got out the maps and the maps were exceedingly accurate and clear but they did not refer to the place where they were.

One of the most maddening things about the British is they never can admit defeat.

For more than four hours they searched the woods and voisinage. And then their diligence was rewarded for at last they saw two men and two men armed with guns. The general halted so did every one, and they held a conference on what should be done. It was quite simple. Laversuch was to go forward and hail them. There were three possibilities. It was quite simple. When Laversuch said hail they if they were British just disguised as British would say hail. If they were not disguised and said nothing and then ran they would be French. If they were disguised as anything except Germans they would be Germans and they would say heil. It was as simple as that. Laversuch said, and the general very clearly explained that they would be behind him and in the eventuality of the most likely thing happening Laversuch could take his word for it that he would be certainly avenged.

Laversuch said afterwards that what made him keep on going forward was the thought of the general behind him and those behind the general having their pistols loaded pointing at his back. Laversuch said any man would have gone forward or passed out.

Anyway there the two men were. Laversuch was shaking like a leaf. When he got near enough to see he saw the two men too were shaking like a leaf. When he said hail they threw up their arms above their heads and one of them had to be given brandy to make him come round.

The two men were two French gamekeepers. They had been enrolled in a sort of French home guard and they were sent out to look for parachutists and for four hours they had been avoiding them. Then at last they had been caught up by them and had seen them coming towards them, and then well there they were.

When Laversuch translated to the general that he looked like a German parachutist disguised as something British, the general said something and a good deal of something about the

French mentality which you would never suppose they were allies from it.

And ofcourse quite soon afterwards they were not. Which just shows.

8 Béthune
(May 19th-20th 1940)

Sunday morning to Monday midday

As I said, the hunting party returned to Avesnes and at six we went back to Givenchy to get some sleep. Did we need it. At this time we were all that is all eleven of us were sleeping on the office floor and I preferred not. In the size of the office two was a crowd and eleven a demonstration. I slept outside on the raised concrete rampart round the yard of the farm. This morning I did not, it was very warm and sunny and so enjoyable I slept in the orchard. It was lovely. There was a cherry tree with blossom on it and long grass under it and birds in it, it was lovely. It was then turned seven.

Almost immediately there were shouts and confusion and well there was Norris. Great God man he said where the devil have you been we are off.

I do not know how it happened, I was under a tree in an orchard and then I was dressed and packed up and on my bicycle we were off. It was Sunday morning at half past nine.

We roared off north to the St.Pol road and then we were there in the refugees. Well in. They have been described and description is enough but being in them was worse much worse than just watching and controlling them. The dust was limitless. We grinded along in bottom gear, we stopped, then we grinded again. Everything was hot and the engines were hotter.

After an age we reached St.Pol and somehow we got through

it, I stalled going down in the middle of the steep hill going down into it, but somehow we got through St.Pol and the refugees and the frantic policemen where everything was blocked and where everyone was inextricably wedged and the heat and the dust, but somehow we got through and then on, and at last about three oclock we reached Béthune.

It was still Sunday. We were, we had not had any since those bread and eggs the day before, we were hungry. We parked our machines and half of us went to see what there was to eat. We found a restaurant and fortunately with a wash basin in it. We had to be careful where we ate because our money was running short, we had pooled what we had but still it was not very much. We had a meal it was rather expensive but quite satisfying. Then we came back and down a side street we lay down. At the bottom of it just round a corner we came across two hundred Belgian troops lying down in heaps. Why they were there or how long they had been there I do not know. They were lying there in heaps of them. Later on in Béthune we saw hundreds more either lying down in more heaps or walking along slowly in bunches.

Then Laversuch came to say he had found rooms for us with a car park near them. We went there, chained our bicycles to the railings round it and went in to the rooms. They were on the top floor of a ramshackle building over a restaurant quite unfurnished. Two had straw on the floor, two had not, I chose one that had not. The next thing was to try to shave. I found two bottles and some water and I used my billy can. The bottles once had petrol in them. This turned out later to be bad for the billy can because in eating it always had a taste of what the bottles had, but I did not mind that now, I was not eating I was shaving. Laversuch had arranged a very good meal downstairs with something to drink before and plenty of red wine during and then cognac and coffee after. We were a very jolly party and made some jolly speeches. There was a very loud radio and two birds in a cage over it and the radio was first Marseilles and then went Spanish. The meal cost something ridiculously little about twelve francs each I think. Immediately afterwards we went to bed.

Something happened during the night. I forget what but it did not happen to me. Wright Houdret Norris and Crew went off on motor bikes, or perhaps Hyland and Barnes, these were the ones most often in agreement with their machines, they went off at about midnight with Major Watson. I never knew what for and when they came back they had forgotten. It was probably parachutists.

The next morning, that was Monday morning, we went to the Town Hall and waited there. Noone knew what we were waiting for but in the army nobody thinks about it there is so much of it. We sat on the steps and sat on the pavement and sat on a low stone wall. Barnes did most of the talking like he always did but still the others did some, we had some Penguins for reading and Morris as usual was reading his Latin. He said in times like these Latin was useful because it was dead and he liked to be prepared. France bought chocolate and Pound some oranges. It was very agreeable. Strings of Belgian soldiers kept passing through and some French ones. They had mules or perhaps not it was horses they had and guns. They looked very dirty and dishevelled and leaderless. We asked them where they were going. They said they were going to reform. We said had they been in battle. They said no they had been mobilized but things had happened so quickly that mobilization had never been completed so how could they be in battle before they were mobilized. By being mobilized they chiefly meant I think being given arms and perhaps some officers. They walked slowly through the streets with their horses and guns. It was rather depressing. You cannot get anywhere far in modern war by walking slowly unarmed and unmobilized.

We had begun our waiting at nine, it was now after twelve. I went back to the restaurant and ordered bread and eggs for half past. Then at half past Major Watson said everyone was to leave Béthune at once. I went to cancel the bread and eggs. An airplane came over. There was a loud bang and a column of smoke shot up at the end of the street. There were more bangs and then gun fire and then a spiral of black smoke in the distance. I got back to the others and then we left Béthune.

Almost at once we were in the refugees again. The road was long over a wide flat plain and as far as the eye could see there was one long line of serried refugees. We were meeting them, so our side of the road was a bit clearer but still it did mean crawling and grinding.

We had orders to keep at a distance of so many yards between the man in front and behind. When the man in front made a sign we had to stop and when he made another sign we had to cut out our engine and take some cover if we could. We stopped often for ages but we did not take cover.

Then suddenly we got a move on and very soon we turned left off the road and rushed our bikes off it and lay down under some trees. Almost at once we heard a plane and then we heard its machine guns. It was machine gunning the road we had just left and machine gunning the traffic blocked refugees. It maimed lots.

We lay in the shade of the trees. The plane went on and we watched it bomb Béthune. There were two planes doing it. We thought of the Belgian soldiers slowly walking through.

We felt disinterested.

Someone produced out of the car some bread and cheese beer and some chocolate, and I think there was something preserved in a tin. We were grateful for what we had received.

It was not that we were callous, we were not horrified nor indignant, it simply was we were disinterested. What was happening was in our consciousness but our consciousness was not registering. We were living in a continuous present and anything in it was equal to anything else in it. Avesnes already seemed as if it had once hardly happened but when it had it was hard to say. Avesnes had happened yesterday. Did we feel it and know it. We could not. We were living in a continuous present and our consciousness was not registering.

Some time afterwards we went on again. We were in a lane now without refugees. The lane circled round Béthune and any of the refugees could have taken it but they did not. Refugeeing is an instinct and in having instinct you do not have initiative. They stayed where they were and were shot and blocked. We went forward very slowly and at widely spaced intervals. Twice we stopped our machines and lay in ditches. Planes came over. Béthune was getting it hot.

At about four oclock we picked up speed and after perhaps an hour's run we reached Strazeele a village on a hill. This was Monday we stayed there till Friday.

9 Strazeele
(May 20th-24th 1940)

Monday evening to Friday morning

The situation was remarkable, the situation of Strazeele I mean. It was perched on a hill and the only hill for miles around, and all below us stretched the great wide plain.

GHQ was in a villa and our vehicles in a brickyard, we were in a room in a café. It was a large bare room with a marble tiled floor. We lived slept ate and read and wrote in it. In the evenings the wife of the owner of it cooked us a very good meal. There was a farm at the back and she killed there chickens for us, and we washed in the back in saucepans and pans, and there was a bucket also. She said the Germans would take what was left so why leave them chickens, why leave them anything. She had a large family of young children and a husband and a brother and was quite unperturbed in her living and being. She cooked, for seventeen of us without warning and without fuss and waited on us single handed and excellently.

I shaved in a stable with a horse.

Strazeele was a crossroads. The refugees were everywhere, all peasant ones now in big slow carts with big slow Flemish horses. The day after we got there the last of the food and drink was consumed and then the shopkeepers shut up shop and joined the refugees. I did notice one thing, the peasants all carried food for their horses. Ofcourse for them it was like our petrol to us but still that impressed me for food is impressive in a time of scarcity and petrol not so much. There was the same air of habit and instinct about these refugees as about the others and the horses were still looking to be the ones with most direction among them.

It was while we were at Strazeele that the tide was turned. The refugees then began coming back again. They could not get any further west because the Germans were pushing north their wedge. Someone told them to go back home to their farms so they turned round and did. The confusion was fearful. And as they had eaten up every thing in their path their condition was desperate. I did feel pity for them then. Their instinct had been reversed and so at last they were becoming conscious of it, it was ceasing to be an instinct it was becoming a disaster and that did make them pitiful. They were at last becoming conscious of themselves. Besides, they had left their farms with the animals on them uncared for, the cows unmilked the chickens loose the calves astray the pigs and dogs locked up. I do not know what did happen but ofcourse one knows what could would happen. It was pitiful.

None of us ever saw any sign of French authority or direction or assistance. Was there any. There were no sirens no shelters no pumps, no clothing centres no feeding centres no rest centres no first-aid centres. Ofcourse there must have been but we never did see them. Perhaps it just was there was no one deputized to make them function.

One of us I think it was, or I read about it, did once see an air raid shelter. There was a raid on and everyone rushed at it and those on bicycles got there first. One of them jammed his bicycle across the entrance. Everyone argued. They screamed they argued passionate hysterical uncontrolled. There was noone deputized to make anything function.

In Britain it is so different. To begin with when disaster happens we have our genius for improvisation to absorb the crucial shock. Secondly we have a natural inclination for law and order which means that in a crisis every one is fairly sensible. This is important because every one knows everyone else is more likely to be sensible than not so there is a general sense of order and not of disorder. Thirdly we have our police and our police embody the average citizen's sense of law and order. In a crisis they remain authoritative and reliable but they still are recognizable as embodying the average citizen at his best and most sensible. This is just what has happened with air raid wardens and fire fighters, the greater the crisis the more sensible they are but they still are really the average citizen being reliable and sensible. In France the police is not the average citizen he is a fonctionnaire an official and in a crisis what happens is he naturally becomes what he really is an ordinary person without much authority if any. In a crisis this is what happens to all officials who are only officials, they become what they naturally are because being simply officials is not enough. In France it was noticeable that when the law and order created officially collapsed there was nothing to take its place. Authority existed in isolated places due not to officialdom but to individual character and so it was in places where there was a capable mayor there was law and order but everywhere else there was not.

Besides all this in France the official law and order is political, the French can not and do not know like the British know that their police and officials will stand firm because they are citizens, the French do not and can not know who will stand firm in a crisis and that is for them what is so terrible. Noone stood firm and nothing could function, and for the French it was terrible.

The second day after arriving at Strazeele the Field Security Section from X. turned up six of them with Captain Hayley and attached themselves to us. They had formidable tales of Z. how it had been bombed. They told us how really they were the only part of the British army who knew what bombing was. We were still disinterested. Houdret and Barnes talked modern painting France talked food and wine Morris read his latin, Crew Wright and Pound were amicable, Parham tinkered at our vehicles, Laversuch thought and did everything for us and Hyland and Norris grew their moustaches, so each was occupied and happy. Anyway we said why be interested in war if there is anything else to be interested in and there always is we know nothing about war. The Section from X. disliked us and we ignored them. Then when planes came over and they did one day, well I do not know about war and strategy but I do know there was a terrific air battle overhead and all hell was let loose. The X. Section dived underground. We watched the fun, it was exciting and interesting, we were thrilled and joyous. And we were immensely inexperienced.

At this time in Strazeele I was keeping shop. We had commandeered it for an office. Major Watson and Captain Hayley visualized I think a string of suspects being brought in and interrogated in some inevitable way when all would be revealed. They and the sergeant-major sat in an inner boudoir and I sat pretty in the shop outside.

In it things were confused. The first thing I did was taking ladies stockings out of the ground rice bin. Then I did tinned sardines out of felt hats. Then boiled sweets from childrens sandals. There were buttons in the lentils and in the sugar bin were what I think must once have been a box of safety pins. The fruit salad was in the underwear. It was an odd shop.

The owner of it was a woman I judged to be old who had fled in a panic. Her panic had affected the kitchen too. She had suddenly fled half way through her meal. There it lay, congealed and lifeless. In the oven was a dish with some thing dark brown in the bottom of it. The most surprising thing however was the number of tea cups. In a shed at the back was a china store large enough to supply the whole of Strazeele. Every cup and saucer had been taken out and lay about dirty and used. I think the water had been cut off for a week so the lady had used at the china store and there it all just was, used up.

I tidied it. It was something to do. Then one day she came back. She was not old at all she was quite young and looked capable and in less than ten minutes the shop was a shambles again. Anyway together we did wash up the tea things, which is more than ever the Mad Hatter did for Alice in Wonderland. Afterwards she showed me why the water was cut off. She had drained the cistern and hidden her wines and liqueurs there. It certainly was a wonderland.

Upstairs in a lumber room I found a painting by her brother it was of a pilgrimage to Lourdes with the cures. It was pleasing and stirring. I brought it to the light downstairs. She said her brother was a priest but then he was not, he was a child of twelve. She said he did not do much painting now but what he did was more accurate and much better. Ofcourse the painting was much more accurate with a child's directness of vision that was so pleasing and convincing. It was like the Douanier Rousseau very much but heavier. She was pleased I liked it but very puzzled.

Strazeele was pleasant on the hill. There was nothing we could do much. We were still in a continuous present with anything in it equal to anything else in it. The CMP's were in a large building it was a school, we ate breakfast and luncheon with them in it biscuits and stew always and always they could not help that. There really was nothing much to do.

There were suspects occasionally. Major Watson and Captain Hayley interrogated them severally and the sergeant-major stayed around in the shop giving orders which nobody took any notice of. I sat in the shop. The suspects were all innocent, dazed dirty and dull.

The last suspect we had was when Major Watson finally went all Russian and from that day on he never really got back to being wholly English again. Once after a rather Russian bout Captain Hayley said very feelingly you know Major Watson is not always simple to deal with he gets so excited. I said yes I knew that. The sergeant-major said yerse quate so. We looked at him and that was enough. Captain Hayley was nicer when you knew him better if you wanted to but he always talked as though speech was not free but a challenge to freedom.

Well what happened was one day at midday they suddenly brought in something which had been found wandering along the roads and they said your papers please, and he said yes certainly and opened out a portmanteau full of them. The papers were written on all over in Flemish Belgian French and something else and not one of them meant what it was necessary to have. So they brought him in. Major Watson rushed over from GHQ and they were closeted together for a very long time.

After nearly one hour Major Watson came out and said all right you men he's all right you may go. So the firing squad went or whatever it was I stayed in the shop. Major Watson retired to the inner boudoir and he and the closeted man began talking again.

He was the most odiously filthy individual I had ever seen, and with so many refugees it was not very easy to be that. Even through the door I could smell him. He was sallow with yellow teeth and was sort of lank in a limp damp way and he dribbled when he talked. What he was ofcourse was a Russian Prince. He had emigréd to Belgium and had become a traveller for a printing works. His portmanteau which he carried was full of samples of printing matter and with the samples were inextricably included the creature's testimonials and his Russian pedigree. In order to produce the testimonials and the pedigree it was always necessary to disgorge the portmanteau and go through every piece of paper it contained.

Major Watson before he went Russian and while he still remained as English as his ancestry allowed him said, yes all right but why not keep the testimonials and the pedigree in your pocket and discard the rest of the abracadabra. This simple gesture of orderly design was quite beyond the competence of the Russian Prince. All right said Major Watson, but the next time you are found you will be found wandering around with these pieces of paper which may mean nothing or anything to a British officer and you will most certainly be shot. Beyond this point they never got.

One of the things about Russian is it never keeps within bounds. Major Watson would say it in Russian the Russian Prince would say it in Russian, then they would say it in French and what was left over they said in German, and then they went back to the beginning again. They had begun at midday it was now half past two and they were back at the beginning again.

The other thing about Russian is each speaker dramatizes his speaking part. They stop discussing they start symbolizing. The play went on. There would be surges of it. Several times the most cordial agreement was reached. The papers would be picked off the floor and packed up in the portmanteau, the door would be opened, good byes would be said in endearing tones. Then without the slightest warning Major Watson would launch forth into a drenching torrent of Russian dialect. The door would be shut, the portmanteau opened, the papers disgorged, French and German would be called to the rescue, and the Russian Prince would await his cue. Then he would take it. He started right from the beginning. Major Watson would give him a good five minutes before joining in. Then they both worked themselves up into an ecstasy of non-aggression and then as suddenly ceased.

It was exactly like a Russian novel where everyone talks at the tops of their voices not about the point at issue, which is perfectly simple requiring a simple action, but about the theory of the point at issue. And a Russian theory as everyone knows is that a Russian theory is repeatedly insoluble. The two men finished up where they began at a quarter to four. The Russian Prince went off with his portmanteau and his papers, Major Watson went off to GHQ gesticulating like Petrushka.

As he passed through the shop he cried out something which sounded like *Vanya vanya ijshnedskaia obolenskopol!* I went on taking tinned sardines out of felt hats. It seemed to fit in.

On the hill at Strazeele one day was much the same as another but we did feel growing a tension every day. We did not know much about the situation, there were no newspapers no letters and no wireless, but we did know that the Germans were pouring through the gap they had made at Sedan, were aiming for the coast, and were spreading north fanwise. We also knew that far in advance of their main body of troops they had mechanized units of tanks roaming at random in the sector we were in. Patrols were sent out frequently to scout and bring back word of them. Rumour was rampant. It was difficult to get reliable information. Two men kept watch from the attic over the shop with field glasses. If they saw any moving grey shapes in the plain below they were to give the alarm and we were to do the skedaddle.

I fancy we were waiting these few days at Strazeele for news of a counter attack. French troops kept on moving through and heading for the 'front'. The day before we left they were taking up positions in the fields and gardens round the village. We could see their heads among the turnip tops.

One curious thing about Strazeele was it was not bombed. Most of the villages round it in the plain below were bombed. We could see a lot of it happening. Hazebrouck was just along the road. Béthune a few miles away was constantly bombed. Great columns of smoke kept rising all round our island.

One of the most uncomfortable sights we saw was one evening three huge German planes hedge hopping below us. They were gliding silently along. We watched them fascinated thinking they were troop carriers. There was something appallingly sinister about them. Suddenly they opened machine gun fire. They were machine gunning a long hospital train in the station and three refugee trains. There was nothing to stop them. Then they flew off, still keeping low, and then we heard the dull thuds of bursting bombs and saw great flashes and then more columns of smoke rising from the plan below us.

In Strazeele there was a large A.A. battery which was very noisy and perhaps effective. Planes came over often and we watched the white puffs of shells bursting well behind them. In fact they were so regularly behind them we wondered whether it was not being done deliberately. However one day a plane was shot down and the German prisoners were brought to the shop. They looked fit happy well-dressed and well. They were no doubt released in a few day's time.

We went down the road to guard the hospital train. The refugee trains had been kept in a siding for three days without food and without hope of getting any. The line ahead was both blocked and bombed. It was feared the refugees might attack the hospital train to obtain medical supplies and food. The machine gunning had not improved anyone's chances of feeling more amicably disposed towards anyone else.

Actually the situation at the siding was neither alarming nor dangerous. It was merely pathetic. The hospital train was magnificent and French and filled with British wounded from the defence of I believe it was Arras. The convalescents were handing out cigarettes to the refugees and filling their buckets with scraps of food. The refugee trains were principally cattle trucks. On the straw lay heaps of men women and children and babies. They had reached that stage of listless exhaustion from which had been subtracted both hope and volition. A woman occasionally cried out for milk. The rest had given up crying.

When I read how these people are being starved by the Germans I remember how first they were starved by the French.

After two false starts the hospital train moved out of the station. The refugee trains stayed behind. There was noone deputizing to make them function, they remained in their siding starving stranded and abandoned.

From the top of our hill we watched the hospital train creeping away slowly and fearfully over the wide flat plain. Its large red crosses marked it out as a specially helpless target, a defenceless easy prey.

10 Loo
(May 24th-26th 1940)

Friday afternoon to Sunday evening

The next day we left Strazeele. That was Friday. Half an hour after our leaving a bomb burst bang in the middle of it. The café where we had slept and eaten was completely wrecked but the family with the capable mother escaped unharmed. That time anyway.

We wended our way north east towards Loo and crossed into Belgium round about two.

I have no recollection of the journey except that it was very hot and very dusty and very long. We hugged lanes and hedges and ditches. There were long delays when we took cover where we could. There was a long straight road with a ditch and nettles in it. A plane came over and machine gunned the fields. We crouched in the ditch. We moved on. Another plane another ditch. It was just long and endless. I seem to remember bumping for hours over deep clay ruts.

We reached Loo on Friday evening, it is a small Belgian township. The Belgians did not like us and quite plainly they did dislike us. This went on and got more so. The Belgians here they were Flemish I think and I should think that most of them were what were coming to be called Fifth Columnists. There were also many Communists.

GHQ was in a modern villa in the town and the police station opposite. We went outside the town first to a prosperous looking farm. It had I remember the kitchen had tiles and brass and lace curtains in it and we were given some stables with hay in them. A moat with green water lay stagnant round the house and stables. We came here for meals stew and biscuits in the open and tea, we sat on the ground our legs dangling over the thick green water. In our stables the smell of pigs and pig manure was very strong. I looked for other animals but there were none though it seemed so.

We had settled down in our hay and smells when the CMP's arrived, all of them. They said they had been allocated to where we were. We were in one of our disinterested moods again. We went back into Loo and through it and then on to a farm with a large barn. This had stalls with straw in them and no pigs it was much better. Laversuch as usual got round whoever was owning anything and very soon we had water to wash in and then afterwards a meal. The people were willing, not hospitable like the French but willing and obliging. The children of the family came in to the kitchen and stared at each one of us. When they made impolite noises which they did very often we knew then that that was Flemish. There were three photogravure portraits of men on the walls and I asked the Flemish woman of the place who were they. She said my three husbands.

We were days in Loo from Friday evening to the Sunday evening, they were beastly and it rained. Noone now had any money. There was not much to buy but I do remember looking in a window at a packet of chocolate and thinking how wonderful it was if it would be. Ofcourse we now think the same about anything and how wonderful about chocolate all the advertisements are of it and the dummy displays of all the other things are very wonderful but the wonderment then was new. Ofcourse we had our evening meal with the Flemish woman three husbands and children and we had stew and biscuits with the CMP's. We did not pay them but we saved up enough to pay for the woman.

We still made our evening meals into dinners and as everyone talked tremendously of everything it was great fun. Houdret Barnes France Norris and Hyland talked tremendously always of everything and Pound had something to say and Crew talked with Wright. The second night Barnes and I found we were taking sides about Oxford and Cambridge and everyone began listening and it became very amusing and it was. Why I looked up I do not know but I did and I then saw the X. Section looking on their mouths open and a look of dismayed bewilderment on all of them. I do not know how it was but we never could seem to remember they were there. Later on after it was all over I got into bed somewhere and someone came into the next bed after darkness and he said, did anyone here meet any one in Section Thirty. Someone said no, why. He said well all I can say is ... by ... Christ ...

After this dinner I went back to sleep as usual in my prison cell. It was very harmonious. William France slept in the police station it was very simple and orderly because he and I were on night duty in it. I had been sleeping in some grass when it rained and they said the prison cell is dry, I said do let me try. Probably it was the most comfortable and certainly the cleanest bed I had slept in since war began except one once I think was in hospital. The best way to sleep comfortably in the army is to be ill and the next best is to be a Flemish criminal. It is most harmonious.

For two days in Loo we had nothing to do. Captain Hayley suddenly wanted everyone to come round the countryside with him on our bicycles. Nobody ever knew what for anyway we went. We stopped on a bridge and somebody waved at us.

Captain Hayley said we will stay where we are till he makes himself clear, you never can trust these people round here. He was not at all clear so we stayed. The sergeant-major then went forward slowly and came back quickly. He said why the waving man was waving was the bridge we were on was most delicately mined. Captain Hayley was very good and bought us what we needed was a good strong drink.

The modern villa with GHQ in it was opposite the police station and opposite it I sat in the long grass or when it rained against a wall with an eave over it. Twice we thought we were going to move and we did not and then on Sunday evening we were most definitely not to move and we did. How many we were I never did know, there was us and GHQ and RASC and CMP and I think some Signals and well I think noone exactly knew, we just increased as we went on more and more of anyone who could. Captain Bell of the CMP's went out one day in his vigorous way reconnoitring and suddenly round a corner coming towards him were three large tanks. He leapt in a ditch and I expect there all his past life came up from the bottom of it. The tanks stopped when they saw him and pulled him out and plucked forth nettles danger from him. They were British tanks but they did not attach themselves to us, they went on Captain Bell came back. He was a singularly competent and charming person.

GHQ was always on the telephone about all of us what we should do and what arrangements could be done if any for all of us.

About the police station, Major Watson was often in interrogating people. Ofcourse probably anybody found trying to leave Belgium was probably a patriot and anybody wanting to stay behind most probably was not. Anyway Major Watson interrogated the patriots but not the police. He was a little less Russian in his ways but not much.

The police I did not like the police. In a way these Flemish police were easier than the French ones because the French police you had to be friendly with and to do that you had to study each one's importance and hear its history. One thing about the singular importance of a French gendarme was how it had always grown at the expense of some one else's importance and so you came to hear the history of every one's unimportance to please them and be friendly with them, but with the Flemish police you did not need to have to be any of that. They did not expect you to be friendly with them and you did not expect to be either so in that way the importance of each one of them did not matter. Anyway it did not matter enough to have to hear it. We were polite. In the office there were the portraits of the King and the Queen of the Belgians. I said something about them. There was an instant of silence. They said something in Flemish. I said what is it. One of them then said in French, when the Queen of the Belgians died Belgium lost her King.

About this time with the tension all round they caught a man digging a sign in his garden for German airplanes and shot him and the police were told afterwards and had to look relieved as though they meant it, about this time I began wondering about nationality and patriotism. We all were wondering a little at this time they were so confused and worrying it was worrying everyone. They did not seem to go together any more. I asked William France I think it was about it. He said it was what you were politically superseded what nationality you had. If you were French Belgian Spanish Scandinavian Italian German or Dutch and you were Nazi it did not matter what you were except being Nazi. And Communism was the same for the others. Ofcourse there were a great many others who still remained what nationality they had but not the vigorous ones nor the crafty ones. It was worrying. We did not then know about England about the vigorous ones nor the crafty ones, we did know about everyone else and there was no exception in all the other countries there was no exception and that was worrying. Are you your nationality first and if not why not.

Nothing is as absolutely simple as that about nationality and why not it goes back further. I have been thinking about the religion everybody had because religion is like nationality, everybody had it once and then everybody tired of having it at once. Well yes. Everybody had religion once and then they became conscious of it and that was the beginning of the end of everybody having it and certainly the end of everybody enjoying it. Everybody became conscious of it and then immediately everybody began fighting for it and everybody began torturing everybody for having it. Everybody had religion and then everybody had to have religion and then everybody had his religion. After that quite naturally after that everybody died for his religion rather than let anybody else have theirs. Queen Elizabeth was the first sensible person to see it was better to live without religion than to die of having it. They called it freedom of conscience it became nobody's business and so the English Church began its living. Once everybody became conscious of their religion they fought for it and tortured others for it and then they stopped enjoying it and then they tired of having it. They had meetings and movements and revivals and sects and conferences and resolutions but they never could forget that they knew that they had had it. That is why religion is like it is and nationality is like it.

Noone knew they had nationality until they were conscious of it and then immediately they fought about it. You had yours they had theirs and all the others who did not know about it, they were called natives and backward races they were told which nationality they belonged to and so everybody then had theirs and had their nationality, and then they fought about it. The Americans and the French were the first to have revolutions to establish their identity they each made good revolutions big enough to make them conscious of their nationality. Later, in 1848, everybody had their revolutions and then everybody had their nationality their identity and their consciousness of national identity. We had not, the English had no revolutions of nationality or identity we had our revolutions of divinity and kingship. We were different. We said everybody who had a revolution was a foreigner because everybody knows we do not have revolutions so everybody not a foreigner was British we said. We said so and in those days what we said well we just said so. Last of all to have their nationality are the Irish and it is too bad really much too bad that nobody has given them a revolution for it. Still they do what they can.

But nationality is like religion once everybody has become conscious of it and has fought about it and persecuted others for having theirs then they stop enjoying theirs and then they do become tired of having nationality. When little thirteen year old Maud Mason wrote her Jubilee essay in 1935 and wrote "The people in England ought to be proud that they are British, England is better than any other country" there was an instant uproar. The Scots the Welsh and the Irish became conscious of their nationality, they were not willing to let anyone else enjoy theirs and the politicians who want everything like nationality and identity to be political saw their way to making political capital out of it so there was an uproar. They called England being better than any other country old fashioned imperialism. Naturally little Maud Mason was not being imperial nor even being national she was feeling patriotic. Anyway as I said nothing is absolutely simple as that about nationality and why not it always goes back further and deeper.

In Naziism and Communism what is interesting about them is they have had their revolutions and they are in them like religion and nationality. Everybody has become conscious of them and everybody is fighting for them or against them and torturing everybody else for having them or not having them, just like in religion when everybody died for his religion rather than let anybody else have theirs. So what next. Will everyone stop enjoying having them and then get tired of them and will there come to be someone sensible like Queen Elizabeth and see it is better to live without them than go on dying for having them.

In human affairs anything sensible takes time to happen next but in time yes it does happen next.

As I said, there was little to do while we were in Loo. We had time to sense the treachery and disillusion and disintegration all round us and to wonder about religion nationality and revolution. We knew what was happening in Norway France Belgium and Holland but what would be happening in England. We did wonder whether when it came to it everyone would be like little Maud Mason saying the people in England ought to be proud that they are British, England is better than any other country. We did not doubt it but we could not help it worrying because in human affairs anything sensible takes time to happen and time was running, running out.

PART FOUR: THE ENDING

11 Dunkirk
(May 26th-28th 1940)

Sunday evening to Tuesday morning.

We were having our last day in Loo. We did not know we were having our last day it was Sunday. It was a day of long waiting and much tension. There was a lot of bombing all round us of the roads of communication. Once we were assembled to go and then we did not, we had our dinner in the Flemish farm and lay down in our straw in the stalls of our barn. We had our bicycles in the barn with us, they were useful for turning the head lights on to see us undressing by and then any repairs and then always they were kept ready full of petrol. We lay down and then we were told to go, and this time we knew we would go, we did go.

It was dusk. We assembled in the town square and were given a list of villages we were to pass through. We memorized these and the list was destroyed. If we got separated we would know where to go to and where to ask for. We were a great many of us. I forget the order of the procession it was very involved but it was sorted out and we had our places in it and our machines were moving, at last we began moving. Did we know it was our last journey, yes somehow we did.

We left very slowly out of the town square and took a circuitous screened lane and then we changed direction and then somehow we were on a big main road. I do not know but I think we went circuitously for the purpose of confusing the Fifth Columnists they were everywhere and then there was I think something especially sinister about the police, I forget what it was whether we had evidence of their activities or someone had said something anyway there was something it was not nice.

We went along the main road it was getting dark now for

about a mile or so and then a cross roads and out of the cross
roads was coming a convoy. We stopped that is our convoy
stopped. The other convoy crossed ours it was very long and it
took some waiting for. It was sinister and mysterious and a little
awe-inspiring all these convoys creeping slowly through the
night like hunted creatures seeking safety in the dark. It was
dark. Ofcourse we had no lights we could not use them. We went
on slowly in our places in the convoy.

Then I forget what happened next I broke down, my machine
was very bad yes it was very bad, it was the bottom gear all the
time grinding away in it that was the trouble. I stopped and
Laversuch in the car and Parham who was the mechanic
stopped, they did what they could, we went on the others had
gone on, some way on. It was not nice driving very fast to catch
them where they were in the dark and suddenly there they were,
they were all spread out in the middle of the road, they had
stopped. Captain Hayley had his place in the convoy at the head
of our Section of motor cycles, he was in a car ofcourse and
Laversuch was in a car at the back of our Section. Captain
Hayley had missed in the dark a turning the rest of the convoy
had gone along and so now we were lost. We turned back and
followed him on. It was dreadful, the dark was it was dreadful the
dark, it was really it was pitch dark and those long French roads
with thick avenues of trees each side of them was making the
darkness pitch dark. The constant looking made our eyes water.
We went on and on, sometimes slow sometimes faster, noone
quite hitting anyone but everyone nearly hitting someone.

After it was over I have often heard it said this night journey
was the worst part of anything we went through. There was
nothing to measure it by nor anything by, it just went on and on
and the anxiety of hitting someone and the anxiety of breaking
down and the anxiety of keeping on the road you could not see
in the dark, and the pitch darkness of everything.

Captain Hayley was worried. We were in a maze of lanes now
and small villages and none of them had any names. He had a
map and a torch and compared it with the signposts when we
came to one. It had been raining and the lanes were muddy and

that made them slippery, you could not see it but you could feel it slipping under you in the darkness.

After a long time, about two hours, we got on to higher ground with fewer trees and it was lighter. I do not know when it began but it was about now we saw right ahead of us a column of thick black smoke coming out of the ground. It was this that was making the darkness. From time to time there would be quick like lightning flashes and then deep slow red burning glowing flashes. We did not know it then it was Dunkirk beginning burning, the burning oil storage tanks.

We were on higher ground now, it was very desolate, flat desolate and marshy and then before us always the thick black smoke coiling from the ground, and the deep slow burning redness. It was yes it was weird. The redness flared up in boiling flashes, we would all be red like bathing in blood red moon light. Then it would die down, but we knew it was burning, it was always burning and the thick black oily smoke was always coiling upwards in smooth belching spiral columns.

We got nearer to it.

The last stages of this nightmare journey I remember we had caught up with the convoy and we had stopped our mad blind anxious racing. We were now stopping and starting and then spurting a little and then stopping. Every time we stopped we stopped our engines, we had to, and then mine would not start again. It meant kicking and priming and kicking and over again and again. If you get tired enough you can not get more tired. The machine Barnes had broke down and he abandoned it and that was our only casualty.

We were going past a long canal. At last we crossed it and then we all stopped and then there was a steep lane with very deep ruts in it. Up this we went. It was now about two in the morning. Then we came to a field and then there were orders and directions and the convoy dispersed themselves and there we were.

We parked our bicycles in a line by a ditch in a field. There were messages about sleeping arrangements where we could but they were confused. I found some straw by a house in a field, I took off what I could and lay down it was lovely. Wright came later and I think Pound. I slept.

I woke up suddenly. There was a fearful noise. There were planes over head dropping bombs and anti-aircraft guns firing at them. The bombs were not near. I lay there, it was lovely, the sun was warm and shining and after the darkness it was lovely. It was five oclock. More planes came over and the same thing happened. It was very noisy. I got up to look around.

The straw I had been lying on well it was not exactly straw. There was a stable up against it. I looked in to the stable. There was a sort of hurried noise. Two women and a man got up from where they were lying. We were all of us as surprised at each other as each was. They were refugees. They said they had heard the convoy arriving and as it was troops they had hidden themselves and kept very quiet. They did not know we were British troops, they said. They gave me some coffee which was welcome.

I went back to the motor bikes. Everyone was active. We packed our blankets on them. Someone said there was some breakfast going in another field. We had some tea biscuits and jam. There were some trees and high hedges and all among them were packages and packing cases, cars lorries bicycles. We were all mixed up. Where I was having my breakfast an officer was there shaving himself.

When we went back to our bikes more planes came over. We lay down under some brambles. We reached our line of bikes and more planes came over and we lay in the ditch. We were widely spaced and as camouflaged as well as we could manage to be. We just sat and waited. Planes came over and we lay down in the ditch and then we came out of it. We sat and I read Decline and Fall, not Gibbon but Waugh.

A quarter of a mile away, we could see it across the fields, was Dunkirk itself and the planes coming over so often were German planes bombing it. We watched and saw it all. We felt impressed. The burning oil depot was away on our left, the flames not visible in the daylight but the smoke was, it was still thick black and oily and was blowing in our direction. We watched a steeple in the town opposite us and wondered when it would get hit. We never saw it hit while we were watching it.

It was now half past nine in the morning. Dozens of planes kept coming over us. We counted twenty five together once, and then there were more and continually more higher up above the haze. They dropped their bombs on the town. Occasionally we heard machine gun fire. British fighters were up there one against twenty or thirty or more. Once a piece of metal floated down from the skies at our feet. It was painted an egg shell blue.

Dunkirk was burning.

In the field by our ditch peasants were working the soil. Some times a German plane would come low down and machine gun them. They lay down flat, we crouched in our ditch. Once we saw three German planes gliding just over the fields, looking for something to fire at. They killed some animals but luckily not in our direction.

In the fields around us the earth would shoot into dark showers. Spirals of black smoke circled the near horizon.

At the end of our field was a farm house. They offered us coffee which was very good and very good of them. These people were perfectly calm. The peasants in the fields never even glanced towards Dunkirk. They seemed quite indifferent to what was going on all round them. And all over them. The men and women were thinking only of their crops. How much better they were than being refugees, and yet such indifference such utter indifference, was it a sign of a virulent people defending their homes from an evil enemy.

Soon after eleven we moved our bicycles in to a field with better cover and bigger trees and a deeper wider ditch. The raids grew more intense. We thought we should be spotted any moment. Great black bunches of smoke and rubble were bursting up from Dunkirk. It was not many hundred yards from where we were lying. The ground shook. We crawled under lorries.

Then the order came to destroy everything. Everything. We smashed our bicycles up with hatchets. The radiators of the lorries were smashed in and then their engines were smashed in. Our blankets and ground sheets we threw in a pond. We could not burn them for fear of being revealed.

We were told to take what tins of food we wanted. I took two packets of biscuits and a tin of milk. There seemed to be quantities of food to be destroyed. Everybody was destroying everything. It was not exhilarating. No it was not exhilarating no it was not it was curiously hurting us to be destroying so much of everything.

In the middle of the area of destruction I saw a figure seated on an upturned empty packing case. He was holding his head in his hands. He was not looking but he was hearing it all happening all round him. He was looking not quite miserable but dejected, quite dejected. It was the Brigadier. Near him his driver was smashing his car with a pick axe.

I nearly did say something to him. After all if you are an adult you can say something but then if an adult why say anything. I did wonder what did it mean to him. Had he had hopes of glorious deeds, of achievement of valour of planning and success. And they had come to this. And then I suddenly did realize what he had been going through. I remembered the telephone ringing at Loo, and how it must have been ringing at Strazeele, and then at Béthune and all the way back to Avesnes, the telephone ringing every day. He had had the knowledge and therefore the anxiety of the dangers, and then he had had to steer us through the back lanes and through the back villages avoiding air raids and machine gunning and traps and tanks. Who had decided just when to move and when where to move to. Who had maintained communications. Who had planned the whole complex organization of moving through difficult territory perhaps five thousand or ten thousand troops and non-combatant troops, who had worked and planned and achieved it all out?

As he sat with his head in his hands, on the upturned packing case in the midst of the desolation, did the brigadier then know just how slight were the chances of rescue.

Anyway there we were all there. He had done that. The rest was beyond his control. We did not know it but he must have known it sitting there with his head in his hands. Did he think it was the end. Did he survive it or not.

At twelve we piled in to a lorry and were driven off into the town.

We stopped where the houses began got out and walked. We still had our full equipment on us. We walked for about a mile along a cobbled road, a canal with a steep bank down to it on our right hand side. When planes came over we jumped over the railings and threw ourselves flat on the bank.

After each raid we resumed our walking. There was noone to be seen but ourselves. We were surprised to see the houses still standing, they were but hardly a roof was intact and not a single window. As we neared the centre of the town the damage was greater.

Laversuch still had the austin car. He gave us lifts in turn two at a time. We reached a place and collected there. The car was abandoned. We joined the stream of troops and walked on into the town.

We came to a wide open cobbled space by the docks and there we sat down. The raids had temporarily ceased. It was one oclock. A short way off a warehouse was blazing. There was a continuous sharp crackle coming from it. It was a store for small arms ammunition. There were other fires burning near by too.

We walked through more streets. They were full of broken tiles and brick ends. We passed some groups of burnt out searchlights and smashed up A.A. guns. The town was defenceless, all had been destroyed. We crunched glass under foot. The shops stood deserted, their contents strewn higgledy piggledy on the cobbles and pavements. We reached a big open space of sand dunes. It was dotted with troops. We sat down in the sand.

The sand dunes stand at one end of the town. They are enclosed on three sides by houses, on the fourth side stands a gasometer. At the eastern end which we now were facing runs a canal or river spanned by a bridge. The road over the bridge runs through the dunes and leads on to the esplanade and beyond it to the beach and sea. We could not see the sea. We were now in the sand dunes at their western end.

We were talking about what should we do if an air raid came. We joked about it. There was abandoned a bread van near us. We said we would get into that and get baked. Somehow out of the sand appeared Major Watson. He stood up and looked like a man being busily engaged. He put it on. He proceeded to put on a bright dress forage cap. It had green on it but it was mostly vivid orange. We stared. It was the kind of cap you keep for putting on. He put it on. He started walking about in it. He was very Russian. He is looking for the ballerina, we said. We did not see him again. We said what food we had selected to bring with us and we showed it round and compared it. Pound produced a tin of tinned beetroot. We were much astonished. Pound said he liked beetroot and anything was nice for a change but particularly tinned beetroot was nice and beetroot was nice for a change. We let him have it. We did laugh.

Just then we heard planes coming. They came very quickly. Some of us got into the bread van. I stayed where I was in the sand to see what would happen. It began to happen in a moment.

The planes came right over the dunes and dropped a stick of bombs and there were more of them and it was so quick. I watched them burst by the bridge and come tearing across the sand to where I was. I lay flat and waited no not waited I lay flat and prepared. The first stick ended, there was a dreadful pause, the second stick began. The bombs came swishing down. The first crashed into a building not fifty yards away, the rest ploughed on. The raid was over.

I can see now those bombs tearing across the sands in a line towards me. I had never visualised speed before. It was like a new colour, indescribable.

The raid was over in what in ten seconds. In those ten seconds we suddenly knew what war was. We had not known it before.

We searched for cover. Opposite the building that had been hit we found a cellar. There was not a moment to lose. All the houses had big cellars and all were full of soldiers. We were the last to be admitted to this one. They put a ladder up to street level through the grating for us. As we were climbing down another raid came. The bombs crashed down, we were covered in dust. We fell into the cellar, pulling the ladder after us and shutting two iron shutters.

We stayed in the cellar for some hours. The raiders came over about once every ten minutes. There seemed hardly a break in between. They were using screaming bombs and incendiaries. We soon knew which bombs were near, which not so near. We crouched against the walls. It seemed an eternity before the screaming ceased. We heard a bang or a thud down the street followed by the empty brittle sound of falling masonry.

After a while the raids eased off and we had them every half hour.

It was in a way rather hopeless being down in a cellar not a deep one. Sometimes we just felt if it would stop for a moment, just for a moment, raid after raid if it would just stop just for a moment. We stayed where we were.

France and I went exploring. At the back of the cellar we found a banana store with hundreds of bananas hanging there in bunches. I am fond of bananas. I ate about fifteen. We found some sacks in a corner and we lay down on them. We were thirsty and we shared our tins of milk.

After some time we heard that is we had for some time been conscious of it but now we clearly heard the sound of walking footsteps in the street above. Those in our cellar asked what it was. An order had come that all soldiers were to proceed to the dunes. We wondered why the dunes why go in the open. We stayed where we were. The footsteps though were incessant and they worried us, the raids had lessened and that reassured us. We still could not understand why the sand dunes but if everyone was going there why we would go there. Actually the order had been confused, it did mean the beach not the dunes and then gradually we did all go to the beach, but not yet.

I forget now what happened, it got to be confused. We were some of us were separated and two went out from our cellar to tell the others to meet us on the dunes. There was instantly a raid and a fierce one, we stayed in the cellar and the others were separated.

After the raid I said I would go to the dunes and find them, the dunes were quite near two hundred yards beyond the end of the street. France came with me. While we had been in the cellar the street had filled up with debris. It looked wretched and desolated. There was smoke and burning and a thick haze. It was like a film of desolation. We knew it and saw it, we could not feel it but we saw it and we knew it was happening. The troops were walking along and on, hundreds of them. We walked to the end of the street.

As we reached the corner where the dunes began we heard more planes, we did not wait we just rushed below to where we could. It was horrid. It was not much below and thin walls and everything I do not know what it was it was horrid and squalid. The planes went over and then more planes and then the screaming again. There was an awful noise. Three soldiers came tumbling from somewhere, they looked shaken. We were crouching in bottles and then more screaming and it got louder much louder and we knew it was coming and we could feel it coming near much nearer and. I shut my eyes. The explosion shook everything. It was horrid, but we were alive. It was horrid. We waited and then we got up. We swallowed, it did make us dry this sort of thing ofcourse it was the shock. The three soldiers they were so young and so good, they were rather white and so young they were being so steadfast and plucky. They said they had not eaten since yesterday. I said I had and luckily I had some bananas. They had them.

We went back to our first cellar and met everybody coming out of it going to the dunes. And immediately there were planes coming over. There was no time for anything. I rushed at a door and I was in a big hall with marble tiles and lots of glass roofing. I threw myself down in a corner. The bombs were already coming we could hear them. Two men dashed in and threw themselves near me. We lay there panting pressed to the marble tiles. The bombs screamed over head. It was odd how you could tell them as soon as they began how near they would be. We listened intently to the sound that they made. We were sweating hard. Four went whistling near but over us and then the fifth. We heard the fifth and we knew it was coming. It was a matter of seconds I suppose and yet it seemed eternity. Sweat streamed off me. I read once a story of a man caught in some points by his ankles and the night express was due and he heard it, screaming and roaring as it rushed towards him and he was caught in the points by his ankles. It was like that. I said this is the end, let it be over quickly let this the end this is the end and let it be over quickly. Please. The scream plunged downwards there was a shattering crash and the ceiling fell in.

I only said that once that this is the end and let it be over quickly.

The bomb had missed us by yards. As we picked ourselves up we saw through the door the building opposite in ruins. It was burning too. The other two men were Crew and Norris.

We made for the dunes to meet the rest. They emerged from holes in the sand that is Wright and Barnes did and Hyland the rest were separated. They had a message from Laversuch saying where the rest were, it was over there. Noone could remember what the message was exactly and noone knew where to go or what to do. There were troops everywhere. Noone could give any messages or take any messages it was all puzzling. There was something about a dog. Noone could get it quite clear what it was. It was all so puzzling. Everybody was moving and everybody was saying it was better to stay where they were and better to be moving elsewhere.

We knew our ten minutes were nearly up and it was time for the next raid.

I remember everything quite clearly but it was so puzzling like it had no reality. It had reality but it eluded being dealt with.

I said I was going over there to the other side to a big dune. I could see some bushes and anything I thought anything to get under something. We went off Wright Barnes Norris and I think Hyland. We had just got there and our ten minutes were up and the planes came over waves of them. It was not now escaping it was just would we be missed this time. They were aiming at the gasometer and the gasometer was just behind our dune. They missed it and they missed us.

We now saw the soldiers streaming down the road over the canal bridge making for the beach. I said come. They did not. Later they did but not then but Norris came and we joined the soldiers on the road. Everybody knew, it was instinct, that we must cross that bridge before the next raid came. We hurried but it was some distance off. We hurried and we got there and as we got there we heard them again the planes were coming again. We raced across the bridge and we got over and I hurled myself through a privet hedge and we were in a wood. We lay on the earth panting and sweating. I was by a tree trunk and Norris just behind me and the road just in front of the privet hedge in front of us. It was the worst raid. It took longer because there was more of it. I do not know how many bombs came down they seemed to be everywhere, they just came down, and screaming down. It lasted about forty minutes. It did not seem longer or shorter or like forty minutes it just seemed to go on like it had been going on.

We lay with our faces in the earth sweating.

I remembered, my mind was extraordinarily clear I remembered I did not feel fear. I do not think any of us did. I remember thinking I did not feel fear and then wondering if my sweating was not after all just fear. Was it. I was thinking strongly. Time seemed suspended to be standing still. I thought, I will not be killed I will not be killed I will most certainly not be killed like an animal like this in a hole like an animal and like this. I said I will not be killed, I will not be killed I have things to do I will not be killed like this I will not be killed like this I have things to do like this I will not be killed like this. And then I felt yes all the indignation and yes all the humiliation of it that there we were there lying like animals there in a wood here and there they were dropping things on us up there to kill us like animals were down here. It was the humiliation of it that that is what war had come to and man had come to war. There they were up there in machines up there and they pushed a button and we down here we lay close in the earth crouching like animals but we were not animals, we were living human beings and they pushed a button in a machine and nobody knew it if we were hit or dead or if we were living human beings if we were living human beings why know it it does not matter and you can not hit back.

So we lay there and they pressed a button and the indignation and all the humiliation of it.

We none of us were hit and the bridge was not hit. We got up and walked through the wood. When we saw what its use was being we were glad we had not been hit. The wood was an ammunition dump.

It was a long walk. Everything was terribly confused. You could think clearly inside you but not outside you. It was shock ofcourse. Later on you could think outside you but nothing responded from inside you, and that was tiredness. We walked on. Everyone was separated from everyone else. We were now Norris Hyland Crew myself and later somehow Pound.

How we got to the beach I do not remember but we were on it and noone knew what to do. Noone gave any orders and noone knew what to do. There were no officers. Later on we saw some in a room smashing windows to avoid splinters and they said we were to wait on the beach and keep out of sight. We got in to a bomb crater in the sand about fifteen of us.

It was now seven oclock and then the raids somehow ceased and there were no raids until nine. I do not know how this happened. They said it was their dinner hour. I expect it was not it was the RAF had beaten them back. We were feeling a little about the RAF not being there. Feeling helplessness is dreadful and not retaliating and you do quite naturally wonder why you do have to feel it and we had been, we had been feeling help-lessness and not retaliating and so much of it. Now ofcourse the RAF has been explained and there can only be now thankfulness for what they did and were doing, and praise and marvelling at them for how they could ever do it.

We sat in our crater. Someone had a portable wireless. Soldiers do retain strange things through all adversity. He turned it on someone was making a long speech about something we did not listen to it and he turned it off. We had some biscuits and someone had a bottle of rum and we each had a pull from it and we shared out cigarettes. Everyone chatted, not much I forget what about. I think we were all thinking about going to England if it seemed only to be possible and we were all hoping each one his thoughts. We could see the sea.

It was rather far out and very still and no waves. It was grey.

There were wrecks in it. There was a French destroyer absolutely in half in it. We watched the sea and thought of England and how wonderful to be possible. It was very still.

Now the raids had ceased we began to notice other sounds. There was the continuous crackling of the small arms ammunition warehouse, right through everything that went on crackling. And there was the noise now of fires crackling. The town was on fire. The oil storage tanks were still burning and the sky was covered by a thick grey haze. Bits of burntness blew over us and settled on us. There was no haze on the beach but everything was filled with a sense of burning.

We began to want darkness.

After an interval we were told to collect at the top of the beach by the esplanade. We did so. All of us did so we were all of us standing there in thick long lines of us about ten abreast and we stretched to right and left. It was a long line stretching along the length of the beach and as far as you could see it where it curved. It was getting dusk, there were about two miles of us standing ten abreast.

Somehow then there were suddenly marines among us. They were startling and wonderful and we knew it meant a ship had brought them and that was wonderful too. They brought efficiency and discipline, they had officers who ordered them and they knew what to do and how to do it and where to go. Time was a factor to them and they were controlled. They were impressive and reassuring and comforting to us.

We were counted in batches of fifty and sent off in batches down to the sea shore. The first batches lined up by the sea and sat down in the sand, the batches behind them lay down behind them and so on till the beach up to where we were standing was covered in separated batches lying down and waiting.

Row boats would take out the first batches to the ships and then they would come back for the next batches, and so on. The ships, we could not see the ships they could not come in near because the tide then was not deep enough, and there were currents.

In counting the batches I had been separated from the others of our Section and I now was with only Laversuch of the ones I knew. There was no room on the beach so we in our batch and those in other batches were sent under cover in to near by buildings. Ours was a café with a drinking bar. There were tables and chairs and empty bottles and hundreds of empty bottles and every thing was indescribably confused. The mess was appalling, everything was mixed and broken and derelict and just everything was desolate. Laversuch and I went into the back parts to see what escape there would be if a raid should come. There was a kitchen and a small window and we opened a door in to a small yard. We were very thirsty. We found a kettle and it had some water in it and which we drank out of about a cup half full for each.

After a long time of waiting we went out, there was a place for us now at the top of the beach, we lay down. The batches by the sea were being taken off in rowing boats. Gradually we crawled nearer to await our turn. It was important not to stand up and especially important not to make our moving ever conspicuous.

It was now almost dark. We had been praying for the darkness and now it was coming we were thankful. The town was burning the whole town was burning but the flames had not crossed the wide open space of sand dunes between the town and the beach, and the row of esplanade buildings screened the beach and left it in darkness.

And then I do not know how it happened but the flames did come. We could see them coming and the esplanade buildings were beginning burning. Then a big building, the casino I think, with two big towers and a cupola began burning and then there was a rush of flame and we were all in bright red daylight.

We had been praying for the darkness so much it was so much a disappointment to be in bright red daylight and so much to be conspicuous and exposed and there we all were.

After that there was always fire, for hours there was fire and flames and falling masonry and falling glass and crackling and smoking. Fire was everywhere and everywhere was burning.

We just lay flat in the sand not daring to move we were such a target. Would it end.

The raids had started again some time ago. They kept coming over and over, the bombs screaming down over head and sometimes just swishing down. They plunged into the burning town.

They were also dropping mines in the sea. I do not know how we knew that they were but we knew it was true. They were always dropping something everywhere and over everywhere were planes over and dropping mines and bombs were over everywhere. We lay they pushed a button and would it ever end.

The blazing casino had burnt itself out and where we lay we were in shadow now. We relaxed our huddled limbs. Suddenly we heard a hissing noise and then suddenly we were bathed in vivid white light. It was a fearful shock. They were dropping flares. They placed them right along the beach and there they burned in fiercely hissing noises in vivid blue white light. We crouched down motionless, hugging the sand.

Their planes were over all the time. They dropped bombs on the town and on the beach and more flares on the beach and then flares which floated on the sea. Then they came down low and started to machine gun the rowing boats and those who rowed them near us. Would it and could it end and never end.

We lay in the sand motionless. By now it was very wet. The tide was coming in and we were quite close to the sea. When you moved a hand or an arm it made a small light it was phosphorous. We tried in our batches to look like rocks and seaweed, and I afterwards read that that from the sea was what indeed we did look like like rocks and seaweed.

I do not know at all for how long we lay like rocks and seaweed. It was wetting us.

Now began a long period of waiting dreadfulness, it was all confused and there were cries and shouts of men and over everything the lurid light of fires and burning and the bright white light of hissing flares and shapes of black men moving, moving down towards the sea. There was a confusion and a sense of disorder and feeling of not of despair but of something near despair. And there was tiredness, tiredness over everything.

The system of waiting turns by batches had broken down. The rowing boats had been machine gunned and there now were none. There were long long lines of waiting men for a boat and waiting men and then gradually everyone knew there were not enough boats to take any more. Those farthest from the sea came down to be nearer and those that saw them moving nearer then moved too. There was not a rush, there was just everybody shouting and crying to lie down and keep still and everybody just moving gradually forward and nearer and nearer to the sea. Gradually they moved nearer and those nearer shouting to them to go back and everywhere the lurid glow of burning and black shapes of men moving and then men running. They were running to the sea and then, then there were no more batches and no more turns and no more boats. There was crying and shouting and men running and waves lapping and no more boats and no more turns for any one.

I got up from where I lay.

It was one oclock in the morning.

It was cold and chilly and there was much wet sand. I went to the sea and stood at the edge of the lapping waves. There was confusion and everyone was there and noone to tell anyone to do anything. There were men in the sea searching for boats and some some distance out were swimming out to the ships in the grey mist out in the sea. It was cold and grey, chilly and far away.

I walked out into the sea. Why not if this was what we had to do why not and if we had to do it why not walk out into the sea.

I walked out waiting for the cold wetness to come through. It came. I waded on. There were no boats, nothing. Dimly in the greyness I could see some shapes they were ships. There was much shouting in the distance round them in the mist. I waded out up to my knees. I stopped. It was hopeless.

There were men all round me wading in. The sea lapped round our thighs and waists, it was so cold so grey. It was hopeless. In the greyness men were shouting crying plunging on out to the grey dim shapes in the distance the ships in the mist. They were so far away. It was so cold so wet and chilly and so grey it was hopeless. The crying shouting men went plunging on.

Then someone said and then everyone said all the officers had gone on board the ships. They had gone on board and had they gone and we were left there were we left there and noone knew what to do, there was nothing to do we could do. They said officers had gone away on board the ships and we were left there were we left there.

And everyone began walking out of the sea on to the beach.

I think this was the worst moment, I think this was the lowest moment. I thought would there be panic. I thought I must think of something I must think of something to tell them something anything to stop a panic. I must think of what to tell them where to go, I must think of something anything to stop them panic. The officers had gone and left us and something I must think of something anything to stop a panic. And I could think of nothing, I could think of nothing to tell them to stop them panic. I could think of what was happening and what was going to happen but nothing responded nothing, I could think of nothing, not a thing. The officers had left us.

We got out of the sea. There was an officer standing there. He said go to the pier there will be a ship there waiting there. Everyone went off in that direction. There was an officer standing there.

The officers some of them had gone off to the ships, they were in a destroyer and a torpedo came in to where they were sleeping and killed them nearly every one. There were other officers many other officers on the beach but just then we did not see them except this one young officer who said to go to the pier a ship will be there. The officers then we knew the officers they had not gone they had not left us.

We were walking along the beach by the sea towards the pier, it was about a mile away to it. There was hundreds of us two or three thousands of us. It was dark now with a sort of greyness. The shore banked steeply into sand dunes which screened us from the burning town. There had been no flares for a while. I was alone now having lost all touch with the others that I knew.

Half way going to the pier all those going to it now met all those who had been there coming from it. They said no ship was there. They said the sea was mined it had tried to get there but it could not. There was no ship there nor any where.

It was a blow to our hopes, it was a great blow. I then thought was it possible that this was not true deliberately not true. Were there fifth columnists disguised as troops among us to spread demoralizing stories. It was possible anything was possible. Calais was said to have fallen. It was said a party of men had escaped along the shore and had reached Dunkirk. It was said that German tanks were advancing along the beach and German artillery were taking up positions to bombard the town. It was said unless we could be taken off by dawn we would be trapped. So anything was possible. It was said and noone said it it just was being said.

I reached the pier. There was no ship there.

I do not know now what I did do. I wandered about. I went down to the sea and looked as far as I could see and I climbed an embankment of stones and looked and I climbed up other places and I looked and there was nothing to see no ship on the sea.

There was a raid, I think there were raids. I remember thinking they would be aiming at the pier and ofcourse they were, there were big bomb craters in the sand all round it and I do remember one was a new one came quite near, it was new I knew because no water had collected in the bottom of it. Yes there were raids there must have been because I remember pressing up against a rock and wondering about rock splinters. Yes there were raids. I was so dreadfully tired. There were raids and raids it was just one long continuous bombardment from the air. I was so dreadfully tired.

Do you know how it is when you have a temperature a very high temperature about one hundred and five or six you lie there and everything is going on. Everything is going on and then you are everything and you are going on it all is awful you are a part of everything and it just goes on. It comes and goes in surges and recedes at a great speed to a great distance and you are with it very far away. You are lying there and you are receding at a great speed to a very great distance and there is a yellow noise like heat and suns in summer. You are a shell on the sea, on the surface of it, and there are troughs and you are at the bottom of it and they enclose you in their heaving folds. There are surges of it and receding and enclosing, you are everything and of it and you do not lose consciousness. You are lying there and everything is awful and you are everything and receding and advancing at a very great speed to a very great distance, like waves on a shell there are surges of it. You do not lose consciousness but you have not consciousness. It advances it recedes it encloses.

I lay on the wet sand and everything was surges of it. I was so tired. My head was on a stone. I was everything happening to me and I could not lose consciousness but I had not consciousness. There was a yellow noise kept coming at a very great speed to a very great distance. I could not think I could only repeat what I tried to think if I could only if only a ship. If I could only if only a ship if I could and if only a ship. If I could only if only a ship if I could only one foot on a ship. If only one foot on a ship if I could only if only a ship. I was so tired. If I could get one foot only one foot on a ship it would be all right because they would pull the other foot after it. I knew they would if only they only if I could. If only if I could. If only a ship if I could.

Like waves folding over there were surges of it.

I felt them kicking me. I had not lost consciousness but I had not got consciousness. They were kicking me. They thought you were dead they said. Two men stood kicking me. It was the tide had come in I was lying in the water.

I got up and sat down on some higher rocks. There was the noise kept coming at a speed from a distance. I groped for it. I concentrated my consciousness on it and dragged it up and held it and asked it what it was. I knew what it was they were shelling the pier. They were shelling the pier. The meaning slipped back to the bottom again. It was too much to mean what it said.

Somewhere inside me was the noise when the gasometer exploded. It was like a large tunnel of roaring sound. It was somewhere inside me and going round.

I walked up over the rocks. It was dawn now. There was a long line of soldiers silhouetted on the embankment. I went to them. Beyond them stretched the pier. At the far end was a black shadow. It was a ship.

I had no capacity left for feeling but I knew it was a ship and the clockwork of my mind went click inside me. I knew if I got on that ship I was in England.

We waited on the embankment. They were shelling it and shelling the pier. I remember nothing about the shells. There were two big gaps in the pier but the structure still held.

They were carrying stretcher cases along it to the ship. At last we filed on. We went a few feet at a time, then we waited. We sat against a low stone parapet. Then we moved on slowly, by inches. We were nearly an hour along that pier.

It was daylight now and time was getting short. I do not know why but we knew it was. I expect it was the tide. We could see now two destroyers. We were half way down the pier. Gradually we began to quicken our pace, and then we were running. There was a part where we ran on single planks over the sea below. It was this getting the stretchers over this had made us move so slowly.

I ran on, the ship was there her bows to the pier. I climbed a small ladder someone hauled me on board and down another ladder and someone said go down, go on down below. I ducked under a rope and ran on. Not down below, no not below.

There was a lifeboat with someone in it and by it a clear space and a post to lean against it. I sat down. I did not mind anything now. I sat down. There was drowning and sinking I did not mind that I did not mind anything now. I sat down.

The captain said through a megaphone to a man on the pier how many more. He said four hundred. The captain said I have only ten minutes. He said four hundred. The captain said all right then if they are there they must come. But hurry, hurry. We manoeuvred alongside the pier and they all came on.

We moved off. It was six or not it was five in the morning. The second destroyer moved too. The sea breezes the sea breezes I swallowed them in wide draughts they were so clean and fresh. We were given life jackets. A sailor came round with tea and a slice of white bread and a piece of cheese. It was wonderful. It did not matter how many of us we were to feed they had enough and enough to feed everyone. The sailors moved about calm and kind and comforting. It was wonderful.

I did not mind anything that had happened. I kept very still. If I moved it might not be. I kept quite still. If I kept still long enough I knew it would be real. It was so wonderful. I was on a ship and any ship yes any ship is England. Any ship yes any ship I was on a ship and on my way to England. It was wonderful. I kept quite still and the sea breezes I swallowed them, no smoke and burning and fire and thick grey oil smoke hazes but sea breezes, I swallowed them they were so clean and fresh and I was alive it was so wonderful.

Some hours later we did reach Dover.

12 England

We disembarked. We crossed the quay over some railway lines and they stopped us there to allow those ahead of us to embark in the waiting train.

It was impressive. The station was entirely empty of people. The long wide platforms stood swept and bare. It was the first time for so long I had seen a large space empty of people.

A long train was leaving a platform full of soldiers. It drew out and then an empty train in the next platform was filled up and that drew out. And then another and another, and another and another and another. The trains filled up drew out and went off. All was readiness and preparation and swift orderliness without hurrying or shouting. We went off. We wondered much where to our train was going.

We passed through I think it was Tunbridge Wells and then skirted London and went southwestwards we passed through Guildford and thought it would be Aldershot but we did not we went right on we then thought Southampton but it was not that either.

Half an hour after leaving Dover we stopped at a small station and there everywhere were trestle tables urns cups tea buns and rolls and sandwiches they were in bags, and then there were helpers they were in clean cotton frocks and they came to us it was needed and we were so pleased. They the helpers they had clean bright cotton frocks and neat hair and silk stockings they were cheerful and smiling not hilarious but normal it was so pleasing. It was seeing them in their cotton frocks and smiling and just as they had been yesterday that made today like yesterday and today like any day. We did not know what was today but they did make today today and then gradually it was Tuesday and that was a pleasure and then we could think of Wednesday and so gradually we could think of yesterday and today and today and tomorrow, and tomorrow and today and Tuesday was today and any day. And so the helpers came and so gradually we became like them we were the same and then at last we were not any different. They had clean bright cotton frocks and neat hair and silk stockings they were cheerful and smiling and they were not it was so pleasing they were not and it was so important to us that they were not refugees. They had been like yesterday what they were today and that made them not refugees and we were not and then at last we were not any different.

The helpers came to us it was needed and we were so pleased. And then they came through the train and men nice elderly men with cigarettes, they had bought cigarettes and they gave them to us. They did everything for us they thought of everything, they were so kind and so pleased and we were so pleased and everyone was kind willing smiling thoughtful helpful and so pleased it was so good of them.

It was so strange. It was like it was not quite really happening but yet it was it was happening and happening to us. Humanity being kind to humanity was really happening it was so strange.

The train moved on. We ate our food and smoked our cigarettes. The sun was shining, it was warm. We sat back quietly. We did not do much talking. It was warm and lovely and the gentle motion of moving was gradual and gradually lovely. Did we doze.

We stopped at other stations I think Winchester was one and people came to us not official people but people and asked us had we everything we wanted and they bought us things, chocolates cigarettes papers magazines it was so good of them. Later there was another country station and more food in paper bags and tea and more helpers and kindness and everybody coming to be helpful and being helpful and good and kind.

We were in Dorset now and bound for Blandford.

I stood in the corridor and leant out. The countryside rolled by. It was beautiful. It was an early summers day, the sun was shining brightly but not harshly. Do you remember what a lovely May and June we had that year. I remember the flowers. The meadows I have never seen such buttercups, they were sheets of gold in meadow after meadow and oxeye daisies spangled them and cow parsley like a bride's veil drifting. It was so beautiful so mellow so peaceful so unchanged. When we got to the camp the next day afterwards the commandant assembled us and spoke to us he said I know what hell you have been going through but here down here in this corner of Dorset we do not know the horrors of war. Think of that when you tell them your experiences. Think of the peace these people enjoy and let them yes let them retain it unspoiled for the few short weeks they may have to enjoy it. Do not spoil it while it lasts. I do not think that we did.

We reached Blandford in the early evening and found a fleet of buses waiting at the station for us. These took us up to the camp. It was a huge camp up on the hills. Young men in blue denim suits helped us out of the buses and carried the things that we had. The young man who was helping me he was so nice and I said but why are you doing this. He said but what you have been through you do want helping. I laughed, I could not help it. It was funny, it was all so funny and so extraordinary and so topsy-turvy to have done something when we had not, we had survived but what had we done, and then it was so funny in the army being given menservants for not doing something. The young man looked upset, he was so nice they were young marines in training to be them and they were yes really they were all charming. I gave him what I had and he carried it and he looked pleased.

He took me each one took one and none of us had to do anything they led and we followed. We filed to three officers behind tables and one took our names and numbers another our regiments and the third our pay books we each were given £1.

There was no shouting and no ordering fussing or confusing. It happened so easily and then we went in to feed.

After that we had showers and washing and after that we went straight to bed. They did not bother us, they left us. They were so good and understanding and so human to have left us. I do hope they will get the gratitude that they deserve.

The next day more trains arrived and the next day more and the next day more. The young marines in training did everything for them and everything for us. They gave up their quarters and their eating times and their canteens and their gymnasiums and they were charming and gracious and charming. For us there was feeding clothing and bedding. Someone told me I forget how many but one day I think they told me they commandeered three thousand new mattresses and they arrived on lorries and one of them I had one of them. In feeding how did they manage the feeding, we had three meals a day and the trains arrived some times at two in the morning and every one had a hot meal and washing ready for them and beds and bedding ready for them. And noone ever made any fuss or shouting or difficulties or confusion.

The others of the Section were mostly in camp at Exeter and there too they had no difficulties or shouting or confusion. Everyone helped every one, that is we did not everyone helped us.

I was I think it was ten days at Blandford in the camp on the hills. And each day was sunny and warm and peaceful. I lay down a lot in grass on the downs. Gradually it settled down and was absorbed and then after a time I could examine it and look at it. Then after a time it lay inside and everything was safe and orderly.

We had done nothing no, had we, we had done nothing. The later trains brought men who had done something, yes they had done something. Did they look it yes they did look it and did they get over it yes they got over it. It was funny how quickly they got over it. They made whistling noises like the bombs falling and they liked it, I did not like it and still I do not quite like it but they they did not mind it. It was funny. Perhaps it was they had more of it and had grown used more to it and so they did not mind it when they made more of it. Perhaps they had got used to it and certainly they quickly got over it. And they had done something for it. And everyone had done something for someone.

I lay on the grass on the Dorset hills under the summer sun. Every one had done something for someone. In England. In France no in Belgium no in Holland no but in England humanity had been kind to humanity. It had happened it had really happened, without fuss and without shouting, without ordering and pushing scrambling debating argument weeping and helplessness and dismay. Every one did something for someone and whatever they could do they did do. Not for honour or glory or profit or credit but simply because they did want to do whatever it was they could do. Every one. The nation. Everyone. The nation. Everyone. Every one did do what it was they could do and the nation yes the nation and everyone was the nation and what a great nation.

It was and is what a great nation.

So that is our story and I will end it here.

But is it the end. No it is not the end. It is the beginning it must be the beginning and it must not be the end. Everyone must be the beginning and the nation and every one in the nation must be the beginning of a new nation and that is not the end it is the beginning.

It must be the beginning that everyone in the nation must begin being a new nation and humanity not for glory profit or credit must be humanity to be kind to humanity and that is the beginning of humanity. That is the beginning that every one does something for someone not for glory profit and credit but simply because they want to do whatever they can do and do it.

They can do and they have done it for the honour of the nation and they can do it and they must do it for the honour of humanity if there is to be a beginning of humanity and not the end of it.

Everyone has done it and is doing it and is it the end. Every one has done it for this nation has done it and if noone else has done it then this nation can do it and has done it and if alone it has done it alone it can do it. It must do it. Everyone must do it. Alone this great nation must do it.

Every one in the nation and everyone is the nation and this great nation must do it and can do it. Everyone has done it for the honour of this nation and afterwards they must do it for the honour of humanity. They must do it. They can and they must do it.

It is not the end is it it is the beginning.

Appendix

Two extracts from 'History and Hope'

18th December 1941

Just today I returned from leave.

I went to the office and they said are you back again I said yes and sat down.

It is curious how they always say it are you back again if you are, for you are if you are and I wonder sometimes do they practise saying are you back again when if you are not. Perhaps not. Still whatever it is does not make much difference if all good things to an end come come when they must it is so.

On the wall is a large new map of the world with flags in the Pacific Ocean.

I said and now I am back again have there been any flaps I said. Oh no they said nothing much really has happened oh yes they said they arrested two Finnish seamen. I said did they and what had they done. Oh nothing said they, we declared war on Finland Hungary and Rumania but nothing much really has happened while you were away.

I sat down and did through some Transport Work Tickets.

It is nice now that the war that everyone now is at war with someone. Up to now it has been a worry how to know what to call it. Everybody knew it was a world war but it was worrying for them to have those staying out of it having their participation so often regraded. The Americans had their participation so often regraded that when it came to it they were unable to believe it. The Americans knew it was a world war but they could not call it so until they had got what was coming to them. So every one now is pleased. The Americans are of course in this like everyone else like the British were the French the Poles the Dutch the Belgians and the Norwegians were unable to believe it or unwilling to prepare it until what was coming had happened to them. One of the curious things about modern warfare is that everyone is much more worried and anxious when it does not happen to them than when it does. When it does and it does not matter who declares it on whom or whether it is not declared at all the important thing is that warfare should happen to them so that they can stop being anxious and start feeling unanimous. It is an extraordinary thing that they cannot feel unanimous that war will happen to them but only when it does that they can when they do. And, too, warfare makes them certain, certain of disaster and certain of victory and certain of what they call justice and liberty will prevail, for certainly once they have warfare has happened to them they are unanimously certain of something. It is an other but equally an extraordinary thing that in peace time they can never be certain of anything at all. So it is nicer now that everyone is at war with someone they know what to call it and it now fulfills our expectations of what a war should be.

It is nice to have our expectations of disaster so fulfilled so often we can take them in our stride. Or is it.

Well anyway I sat down and did through some Transport Work Tickets which had latterly accrued, petrol consumption mileage and speedometers not working and so forth is extraordinarily uninteresting and everything inside was still going round, it is a long train journey London to Inverness and Anthony and everything makes it necessary to be doing something meticulous when they say are you back again and you are if you are. I ticked off petrol with a red pencil and a blue cross against speedometers not working.

My dear Anthony.

Pearl Harbour and Guam. In a way my dear Anthony. And Wake Island. And Midway Manila Mindanayo Malaya. Penang Padang Kupang Madang. Serang and Serong, Tong King and Hong Kong. My dear Anthony. Perang where the meringues come from. What thousands of miles you do have to go to to get anywhere else is it worth it. Well anyway my dear Anthony how furious I still am. Every thing inside is going round and let us sort it if we can. Take living.

In living living if living living in. Take living. If living living in likes living take living living in likes you. I thank you.

It is interesting about living how seldom the pace is the same as it was that is how constantly it is increasing or slowing down and William Galveston said the other day, I have just been staying with him he was saying something about what is called the continuous present because he has just been reading something I have written in the continuous present and he said it allows the most astonishing emphasis to be given when it is necessary even when at times it may not seem necessary because when so much is happening in a few seconds or so little is happening in a few days and you want to say so in ordinary writing one sentence takes the same as any other time to say it if you say so well you say so. In living it is just like that. In living the most astonishing emphasis is happening in a few seconds and nothing for some days is happening makes warfare what warfare is like is the continuous present and this is a continuous diary of what is the present.

When I met Anthony I knew that everything would suddenly begin happening in a few seconds. Then yes it did.

It is strange how you know it with people if they have it or have not, it is just like what I have been saying about living or writing and naturally they are a part of it, in ordinary people anything happening to them takes the same time to happen as anything else whether it happens and they know it or it does and they do not, in ordinary people what happens makes so little difference that they accept it without wonder. But with people like Anthony so much is happening in a few seconds or so little in a few days that the impact is different, so much has happened that they know it and they give and feel it it comes out. I think the difference of what happens to people is not how much it does but how much can they wonder. I heard some friends once ask an army officer what he thought about Dunkirk he said: "Great show. Topping." They waited for something more to come but nothing did it was his description of it. Great show. Topping. Anthony is a sergeant pilot in the R.A.F.

Now just how much petrol has young Evans has consumed. Perhaps it is we are diverging in our methods of addition and

please has anyone seen my red pencil. Oh I think I have counted
these eight gallons in twice over. I mostly find in counting up
anything that is much more difficult than it is when someone
first has done the answer to it that counting up anything in addition makes quite enough as much if it is. It is most disappointing
if it is. I always expect anything to be very much more in addition than what it was but it is not, counting up anything in
addition makes quite enough just as much if it is. Well anyway
has anyone now got an india rubber. Eight gallons in twice over
makes more than enough if it is.

Yes I still feel it, like a dynamo humming with vibrations it
goes on round inside, the trembling aftermath of violent rage.

It is awful to be angry, to be passionately consumedly help-
lessly angry. I have just been this morning I was so passionately
angry and Anthony in the train it was and Anthony I can not do
it now, I will come to it all later on it is war and peace victory
democracy and government the people the future and Russia
and peace and victory, all of it. Anthony said WHAT THIS
BLOODY COUNTRY NEEDS IS A BLOODY REVOLU-
TION. I was so passionately angry. Yes I said. The people and
the future it is their country I said, they must own it and have it
and enjoy it and fructify it and be proud of it it must not it must
not again be democracy and government and poverty humiliation wretchedness and shame and condescension and the vested
interests of magnates financiers and industrialists it must not be
the government and democracy it must be the people for the
people and be proud to be the people. I was so angry. The other,
that is the third one in our compartment the Old Etonian said it
was 'labour camp talk', the government he said the government
were all gentlemen because Churchill was a gentleman and what
gentlemen did was all all right because it was the best anyone
could do for anyone and if not the House of Lords was the aris-
tocracy would preserve and guard our English traditions and
England was always as it had been because they were gentlemen
and they it always would be. It was then that Anthony said what
this bloody country needs is a bloody revolution I was so
passionately angry. Yes I said, and I could have killed with fury,

yes yes I said it does. We shook hands.

So much had happened in a few seconds.

Now I am doing my Transport Work Tickets. It is racing round inside me the rage and frustration of it and Anthony racing round, racing in a Hudson bomber over the wide North Sea. When I am calmer I will tell you about him. I can not do it now till the impact is different and I am calmer to meet him and tell you about him. Anthony, Anthony is valuable.

Democracy versus the people, it is strange and awful can it come to it. I do not know but I do know now the sudden passion of it I could have killed with fury is so strange and awful. Is it why is it. It is all bound up with everything you are, history and hope, and progress belief inevitability humanity, it is compulsion. It is something evolving that makes the present the present and you know it. You breathe it sense it accept it and then someone slams a door in your face and suddenly you are thwarted. The rhythm of your being halts, stops dead. The current of the air you breathe is cut, switched off. You beat against a solid wall of complacency, experience, precedent, self-confidence, pride, conceit, tolerance and compromise. Their very virtues force you to a frenzy and against their solid wall and slammed door you point and shoot your quiverfull of argument. In vain. No argument can pierce the armour of complacency. The current of reason is stopped, switched off. So you cry: 'Down with it! Down with it!' You do not want to destroy, but you must live and breathe it is all bound up with everything you are that makes the rhythm of the present the present, it is history and hope and everything, you know it. Yes yes you feel it, and you know it.

I must calm myself and get it sorted.

I will calm myself and get it sorted.

I make small ticks with a coloured red pencil and a blue cross against speedometers not working.

Pearl Harbour and Guam. My dear in a way my dear Anthony. So valuable.

And flags in the Pacific Ocean.

It is curious how they say it always are you back again. And you are. You are and there you are it is so.

It will soon be time to put away the office files for another day.

Today. Tomorrow. Yesterday.

Over the wide North open Sea.

19th December 1941

This is a diary and everything I will do it all in all in good time.

In writing a diary it is pleasing to be writing if and as it is feeling it. Let me see.

I have been to London then Bath then and Cheshire Crewe and now in Inverness they said that nothing had really happened while I was away. Yet in London, London looked tidier.

The chief thing undoubtedly the chief thing were the truncated church stumps of their spires as they were there, impressive, arrested, authentic. As they were and so they were there, in London arrested, authentic. After that I liked best seeing removed the railings and men so determined on it they did not chop them down nor saw them through nor blast them down it was very ingenious they drove right up to them in a closed in van and out of it they laid on rubber tubing and then the most determined one held one end of the tubing till flames came out and he went on quite determined and nothing happened. I watched for ages but nothing happened, that is it had happened there were the little stumps where the rails had been but I never saw it happen not the scrunching disintegration of the sawed wrought iron. What I wanted to see was them take them away to see whether if putting them back again was going to be easier. Ones hopes hope not. I expect what they will do will be plant quantities of laurels and just today two men in our street have come round with an air of intention and two measuring tapes it was then that I saw how each section of railings the inhabitants had had not clearly thought them sufficiently obscuring they had planted short sections of privet and laurels on the inner sides of their stretches of railings. Really by looking they have not known for years what they had was sections of laurels or stretches of railings. It is curious when you come to think of it the prudence that propinquity arouses. They have a low stone wall with railings on top of it, then a privet hedge, then if possible an evergreen tree in front of the window, and just in case they still want to hide what they do with themselves they have a screen of net curtains and a large plant pot. It is very curious because anyones neighbours all know what they do with themselves and if they do not they make up something worse.

Well anyway so London looked tidier than the last time I saw it was November 1940 in about the middle of what it was going through. I sometimes wonder whether it was worse for those outside London than those inside because those inside knew what was happening to them as little and as much while those outside thought always it was more than it could be. Also it was worrying how the wireless kept repeating how wonderful morale was and when the wireless keeps on saying that you know it must be pretty bad, that is morale is not bad but the conditions that make it necessary to have to mention it must be bad. It has always surprised me about those times that the wireless could never be allowed to tell the people what they wanted to know. In those times there really was a predisposition to believe the wireless so really just a little of the truth would have done no harm. Ofcourse later on everything that was to come has made the truth quite different, like other things it has retired to prepared positions but in those early days there still were enough who would listen to believe it. At any time of course there are enough who will listen in to talk it down. However the authorities decided on the wisest policy was to cause the greatest anxiety amongst the greatest number. So when they said that London had a heavy raid and casualties were feared to be severe, everybody outside London who had relations inside London feared the casualties were theirs. If they had said the casualties in Twickenham or Tooting were feared to be severe, that would have limited the conception of casualties and reduced the general anxiety to Twickenham or Tooting. The answer to that is ofcourse that the important thing was to conceal from the enemy where they had spent their evening because how could they know they had been over

Twickenham or Tooting unless the British wireless told them so. This it is that makes authoritative answers the sort of answers they are. Nohow, contrariwise.

'Some damage was caused to household property but casualties are not expected to be high in proportion to the scale of attack.' "You've begun wrong!" cried Tweedledum. "The first thing in a visit is to say 'How d'ye do' and shake hands." 'The raiders made off after jettisoning their bombs which fell quite harmlessly in open ground. They failed to explode.' Nohow. Contrariwise. "If it was so it might be, and if it were so it would be, but as it isn't it ain't. That's logic", said Tweedledee. But the fat little men only looked at each other and grinned. No British bombs fell harmlessly. They *never* failed to explode.

So being outside London in those days was a worrying thing. Naturally I like anyone else wanted very much to go there and be in something for a change, I had been for some time on an island in the Hebrides and nothing then had happened for so long that anticipation of what it was like was the only warlike thing around us. When at last my leave was due the worrying changed to would they stop bombing it before I could get there. They did not.

When our train in dragging its way slowly in to Euston station outside the sirens wailed, we rushed to the corridors and put our heads out the windows. This I think was what we had hoped and come for, this the anticipation of what it was and was like. The train jerked on then stopped again. The sirens wailed. The soldiers stood with their heads out the windows, starved and anxious and thrilled for war. We strained our eyes and hearing would it happen hoping so.

Across the rail tracks facing us stood backs of houses scarred by splinters here and there, while over them the barrage balloons like drops of silver mercury hung suspended in the crying air. The sirens' warning we heard their wailing, the sirens of London rising and falling in the pregnant crying air. In a clear blue sky their wailing waved to heaven to beware of mans own evil and despair. Yet who cries pity! Let them do their worst! The sliding harmony sucks at the senses, excites the tissues of the stomach, draws out the insides and rouses all the instincts of defence revenge so that louder and louder they call the men at arms to guard the streets and battlements against this shrieking siege. The sirens of London we heard the first one faintly far away, far away the first one sounded then another and another each one picking up the other and another catching the refrain and tossing it in warning to an other one another, louder and louder the one nearest wailing and passing it on like beacons of tidal sound rising and falling fading and wailing in the rolling vibrant air. Twickenham and Tooting fading and wailing in the pregnant crying air.

The sirens tolled the knell of parting day, a fading future wailing our life's elegy to liberty. Another raid was on. Our train stood very still.

Then we heard whistles blowing it was exciting. We stood with our heads out the windows and heard everything going on, it was pleasantly exciting and we were all very pleased. After all if you are British and the Battle of Britain you are naturally pleased to be British in Britain. The whistles were blowing and men we could see men running in the streets it was exciting. I asked afterwards my sister Caroline what they were, she said oh whistles is when there are enemy planes over head it means danger. Did it. As we did not know it there was no danger.

We got in to Euston and in looking for a taxi a loud speaker kept saying Take Cover Take Cover everyone will please Take Cover Take Cover every one will please Take Cover. I went to the place where they book sleepers and did it, it was rather noisy and quite soon over. This was London was all right.

I asked my sister Caroline about taking cover was it necessary or propaganda, she said it was not necessary but at midday it was often advisable and Saturday mornings were the worst, once she had heard the swishing noise and dived for shelter and once she had not and she had never heard anything louder in her life. 'I thought my head was blown off' she said. 'And when did you not think it was blown off' I said. 'Oh' she said 'when I began again to remember what it was I was going to do, I went to a shop and I said "I want three lettuces". It was like talking through a thick glass door.'

When I got to my hotel they explained my room was not quite what they thought it would be. They had put me in a back one. I said I did not mind that but the room reserved for me what was the matter with it. They said there had been a disturbance in it the night before. I said well may I see it. We went upstairs and opened a door stepped in and very nearly stepped right over the other side. I said if they had one I would prefer a room with about four walls and if possible a top and a bottom to it. I am afraid it was very fastidious of me.

My sister in living in a large block of flats lives in a top one. She says though it sways more in really big raids and there is further to fall there is really much less to be smothered under. And she likes the view. We sat there together my first evening and when the sirens sounded she said they were ten minutes late. We had a lot to sit and talk about and it was I do not know quite when when we heard a familiar droning. It passed over head and went off. Then another droning, coming over overhead and going off. There was not another sound. It was funny how the ceiling began feeling thin and I wondered how soon did you get used to feeling the sinister silence and slow throbbing droning. My sister said 'They're coming as regular as clockwork tonight the devils.' Another plane droned over head, it seemed to be cruising the throbbing droned so slowly. Suddenly a gun banged off in a street near by, a hard dry cracking bark. 'Blast', said Caroline, 'they'll start aiming at the damned thing.' And sure enough, we could feel it as though we could see it, the plane turned slowly round and droned deliberately over head. 'Get ready' she said. We sat quite still, taut and rigid, straining to catch the first new sound. We heard it together, the hissing swish. 'Here it comes!' and as she said it she switched off the current, the light the cooker and the fire, and rushed to the shelter of an alcove by the door. Billy dived under the sofa. The bombs swished over head, we heard three crumps, probably in the Park. I sighed with relief. 'Wait!' she said. 'There are two more to come, they usually carry five.' But the plane droned off, its malice satisfied. We sat down, turned on the light. 'I hate these quiet nights' my sister said. 'They make you jumpy.'

Billy returned to his basket. That hissing noise what was it like it was like something. 'It is exactly like a taxi on a wet street' I said. 'I know' she said 'I've often been had.'

'When Billy dives under the sofa it usually is a sign the bombs are near. He sometimes senses it before I hear it. It's funny. When the guns go off he doesn't mind a bit.'

I said 'Why do you go to the alcove by the door.'

'Oh' she said 'there's a girder in the roof. If it gets really chronic I stand in the corridor. They say it's safer, like they say it's only the bomb you don't hear that hits you. Ofcourse noone can prove that it is or is not, but still when it gets really chronic I stand in the corridor.'

'Then you would not know what hit you first, the bomb or the girder.'

'I've thought of that', my sister said, 'I'd just ask God. They say he's wonderful, knows everything.'

We talked till midnight. Single planes droned overhead. It was an uncanny feeling. They seemed to crawl up your spine, up and up till they got to your head, slowly throbbing over, over head. Would they go on. Then you waited till they passed the distance from which you estimated if they dropped their bombs you might be struck. Then you relaxed. Then all over again. I did not like it and I said so. 'Yes' said Caroline 'it isn't pleasant. They say it sounds overhead but really it is not and actually it probably is not. It is the sort of thing one goes on trying to believe in in the hope that some day one will. It is like our being prepared. They always say we are well prepared but everyone not an authority on preparation knows perfectly well we are not. It is vexing. The vexing thing about not being overhead is if it is not it most probably will be. Really anyone not an authority on bombing knows perfectly well how often it is.'

I said good night and went back to my hotel. It worried me

much the strain of everything, the peoples' senses stretched and taut all the time. They are all keyed up. They are on the stretch. They live under terrific subconscious pressure. They are holding tight on to themselves. And they take it as matter of course. What will they when they relax. Madame Freud once said a rather interesting thing about the British quality of being immune to bombs and bombing reactions, she said it lay in the fact of their never transcribing their fear. The quality of fear she said was catching and it was just this catching quality of fear had given Hitler his successes on the Continent. There they had had it and spread it and caught it. But the British had a noncontagious quality of fear because, and this was the secret of their immunity they did not admit it at the time. Why they did not admit it did not matter what it was due to whether pride or self-consciousness honour a feeling of dignity or reserve example upbringing guts phlegm or disdain of emotion did not matter, what did matter was that they did not admit it at the time. Therefore they did not spread it at the time, and they did not catch it at the time. The time was important. It was so interesting said Madame Freud that the British admitted it afterwards, willingly and openly they admitted they had been frightened often badly frightened but by coming out afterwards it was already an objective thing, that is it was harmless not contagious, it had ceased being fear.

I think perhaps it is that and not quite that, there is a little more to it than that. I think perhaps if you are not an entirely British one it is more difficult to understand the difference between victory and defeat. The only thing that matters really being British is there is no choice. The British Empire is not a solid piece of a thing like the European Continent it is a very delicately balanced thing. The defeat of the British Empire does not mean it could go on under someone else, it could not go on like the European Continent until it revived, it would not go on at all it would utterly go. The defeat of a part of it like the British Islands would not mean a political revolution or treachery or being occupied and overrun, it would mean annihilation. If we lose we cease to exist and that is why when we have wars as we frequently do we always believe we shall triumph in the end because ceasing to exist is not as easy a thing to believe in as however frequently the odds are that we shall. In our latest war the odds that we shall be defeated have been so frequently and enormously against us during 1940 and 1941 that in our darkest days it is perfectly true that noone else except only the British thought they would win. They did not think they could win, they simply thought they would win. This was naturally upsetting to everyone else and you will remember how the Americans had to keep on sending their observers over to find out what the matter was. It was upsetting, upsetting to the Americans and of course well naturally much more upsetting to the British, it is a very upsetting thing to the British to be told by observation they are wonderful, they know quite well that being wonderful is much too private a thing to be observed upon and commented upon, they know quite well that being wonderful in the middle of everything has to be kept so private and secure that noone can see it or touch it or say it. Being wonderful with the odds against you is not a natural nor a boastful thing it is something overcome within, one does not tell it one makes it, each one makes and keeps it carefully within. However whatever the matter was and being observed in their having it the British even so still thought they would win, that is we thought so but we could not really think so we could only believe in it. We could only believe in victory because believing in the alternative was quite impossible, you can not really believe you are not going to exist, it is not possible that you cease to exist and believing the impossible is a very British thing.

The person who said 'I think therefore I am' could never be a British one. The British know that thinking makes trouble for them because their thinking is like their agriculture, it is no use thinking ahead of it because when it comes to it it may not happen and when it does may be different. British agriculture is invariably different, that is no two seasons are the same, the next may be worse than the last and in this way it has come to it that as Sir John Russell says British farmers have learned by experience that trouble may come at any time. Nevertheless when it does not they still like to say so. British thinkers have learned perhaps less by experience than British farmers but all the same they know that trouble may come at any time and the next may be worse than the last. And if it is not they still like to think so, for thinking the next may be worse than the last is so like British farming, they have had it happen so often before they have a perfect right to expect it at any time. In this way it is that they have to retreat according to plan, they retire to forward positions for they certainly think they will win in the end because however often that it is they do not, it still is easier for them to believe in the impossible than imagine that they have ceased to exist. The world without the British to run it would be so much worse than the last that really it is quite unthinkable. Well anyway it is unthinkable to them and that is what half all the trouble is about.

Therefore the British do not say 'I think therefore I am', the British say 'I am what I am.' And really the British being what they are has been enough for them for centuries, they do not know what they are but nor does anyone else, they only know it has had to be enough for them to be going on with. When a French ambassador said "If I were not a Frenchman I would wish to be an Englishman" the British ambassador replied: "If I were not an Englishman by gad I should wish to be." The French ambassador thought he might like to be something else but the British ambassador knew quite well he would not, he knew that what he was was enough for any one. And so it is with victory and defeat, the British do not think about not ceasing to exist, they simply know that being what they are has been enough for centuries for them to be going on with. After all if you know what you are you need not worry about reactions to bombing, psychoanalysis, American observers, and all that.

Yet even so. 'I am what I am'. The question is, is it enough and just how many have begun to doubt it. The British have taken so much for granted they have been content to say 'I am what I think I am'. They have not known exactly what they were, nor even where they were, but at least they are beginning now to know how much of it they were not. It is a very disagreeable thing to find out how much of nothing anyone is, but for the

British it is an urgently vital thing to find out what they can do about it before it is too late. It is not too late. The British say it is never too late to mend. The question for them to decide is, how much rust has grown on their needles? Perhaps one day the British will stop saying 'I am what I am' and start deciding 'I ought to be more'. Being what they were has been enough for them for centuries, but being what they are today is not enough for them today nor tomorrow and if other people have discovered it well can you wonder. It is a very disagreeable thing to find out what you are when you thought and were told you were not. Still every little helps if it does. Dear me.

Anyway to go back on that evening I have been describing I worried a little about some other things, I worried that some things were somehow all wrong. They were not what they were, it was a backwards kind of war. Here was I a soldier, living in the Hebrides, in beautiful scenery, in peace and quiet, with little to do, secluded from all sights and sounds of battle. I did not even carry a tin hat, for there was in those days a sort of silly convention it was undignified for a soldier to wear his helmet on leave. Yet there was my sister, in the thick of it, with civilians in the thick of it, risking death, escaping it, facing it, having it. There was nothing undignified about Caroline's tin hat. 'I wear it when the stuff's coming down pretty near but really I wear it because the police will give me a lift if they see its initials.' She worked for far longer hours than I did, for less pay, and in worse conditions. It was all wrong. She did not think it wrong but I I felt it was wrong. They called it total war, and still they do. But really the least they can do in a total war is to let the soldiers have a small share. When will it ever come.

I must say I think the exempted army has borne its anxiety for its fighting women with exemplary patience and calm.

In walking back to my hotel more than anything else just then I would have liked to be a firefighter, more than anything since wanting to be an engine driver. Well actually what I wanted most passionately of all to be was a lift attendant in the Langham Hotel, but that is another story oh absolutely another story.

It is a curious thing how wanting to be anything makes you

always the wrong age to enjoy it. When I got to the age of quali-
fying to be an engine driver I wanted to be a musical composer
and when I got to the age of having to do something for a living
I went into hotels. Then when I had reached the age of hoping to
get out of them I went into the army, and heaven knows what age
I shall have to reach before getting out of that. It is curious
always being the wrong age. I suppose that all the small boys just
now want to be fighter pilots but you can see it happening to
them that they will not, the nearer their age gets to it they tell me
the more they get ground mechanics and Swedish gymnastics.
Even Anthony who is exactly the right age at being a fighter pilot
and actually who is one tells me what he wants most of all to be
is either a ranch in Canada or a chance to make money. I said
'But Anthony surely you have everything, your health and youth,
your courage and valour and all the glamour and the glory of it.'
He said: 'The question is, do you or don't you survive.' So
Anthony being the right age is not it yet, he wants to be able to
be older. How many Anthonys there are, and Anthony who has
everything can all the glory of his youth reach ever the age to
enjoy it. Why not why never not.

Another one I met, I did not like him he was young and
bumptious, at any age he would be bumptious but just now he
was young with it was telling me what a man ought to do in war
he said: 'There are only three things a sahib can go into.' I said
'What is a sahib.' He said a sahib was a white man I said I
thought he was a brown one. 'Well anyway' he said 'there are
only three things a fellah can go into, the Guards, the Buffs, or a
Suicide Squad.' I confess I was astonished. So when I met a firefighter I was prepared for anything. This one I met we were
waiting in a midland railway station for a train already six hours
overdue and wondering whether the station would still be there
when it got to it, but however he was a charming young man he
had been through everything and now was leaving London for a
fortnight's rest. I said it must have been momentously incredible.
'Oh well' he said 'the excitement soon wears off and one fire
looks very much like another as on as above the ground, but on
the ground it makes more mess. Really it is rather monotonous'

he said. He said: 'Yes the blitzes are very boring once you get into them. I want excitement and I have decided now to do minesweeping instead.' And a few days later he rang up to tell me he was doing it. Well really.

So wanting to be a firefighter or an engine driver or a lift attendant in the Langham Hotel or the glamour and glory of an aircraft pilot, what happens when you have them they outgrow you. It is a curious thing how wanting to be anything makes you always the wrong age to enjoy having it when you do. Time it is that marches on. Do we.

By the time I was in my hotel was 3.0 a.m. there were two big explosions. I went to sleep. At 4.30 a big bang. I went to sleep again. The all-clear sounded at 6.0. That finally woke me up. Caroline called in and said: 'I'm sorry your first night in London was so quiet.' 'Yes it was wasn't it' I said. What a dear child.

It was in I think it was in the film called One Night in Lisbon which began with one night in London was the Hollywood idea of what an air raid was like it was most interesting. It gave the sounds of an air raid and the blackout and people walking and talking and in shelters and in parties, it really was most interest-ing because everything was almost exactly as it was not. It was interesting I think particularly that the sounds were not, the sounds were given as the rumble of artillery and the rattle of machine guns and the London sounds of a London air raid are almost exactly not like either. I must say I have never heard the rattle of machine guns in an air raid, in a daylight raid yes high up in the sky in a night raid never and the gunfire does not rumble. That is exactly what it does not do, it barks with a clear hard echo to it, an ack-ack gun in a London street is a very fine sound I do not quite know how I would do it but I think perhaps two French horns an octave apart one open the other cuivré blown sforzando would do it, anyway it is a clear wide strident note not a muffled rumble. In this film was Edmund Gwenn and you could see he was a lord because he lived in one of those American apartments that look like a furnished garage, Edmund Gwenn stood in front of a huge plate glass window and said to his butler in the middle of a raid 'John take this note to the BBC and have it broadcast immediately.' 'Yes my lord' says John and he looks at the note and reads it. 'It is funny John' says Edmund Gwenn 'that in the last war we had to remind the boys at the front to write to their mothers saying they were well, and in this war we have to broadcast to the mothers to write to their boys that they are safe at home.' 'Yes my lord' says John 'it sure is funny.'

Writing afterwards of the night that followed my sister Caroline said: 'As for London, all goes well. We have had a few more bombs just to keep us alive to the fact that the war for Democracy is proceeding according to plan. The sirens sounded half an hour ago but nothing has happened in our direction yet. Since you left, the raids have been much less severe, except last Friday's when it was terrific, just like the night you experienced here. The B.B.C. blandly announced that damage and casualties were not "excessive" in proportion to the scale of attack. I wonder what scale they are working on! However they did not concentrate so much on the West End, it was Paddington, Richmond, Twickenham, Chelsea and Fulham. Richmond has been left in a terrible mess. At one time it was feared the whole town would be reduced to ruins, the fires were so appalling. Then to make things worse, the water main was hit and they could get no proper supply to quench the flames. At the height of the struggle they received a message ordering as many fire engines as could be spared to go to Twickenham, for the place was a blazing furnace. Anyway, in spite of every handicap, I believe all the fires were put out by daybreak. The casualties in Richmond were pretty severe.

'As for the night you were here, I have gathered a little more information now. The London Fur Shop near by Selfridges was burned out, and half of the C.A. next door. Hamptons had its second hit and was burnt. The Carlton, the Ritz, and the Savoy were all hit but none was too badly damaged. Out of the seven hospitals struck I know of only two, one at Paddington and one in Marylebone. A large block of flats out Acton way and some factories were badly damaged. The City and Lombard Street had a big smashing and many buildings were wrecked. Also the

Strand had a good shake-up. Trafalgar Square looks surrounded in craters. The Park is rather sad-looking in places, two bombs fell on the edge of the Round Pond and very many trees have had their branches smashed.

'Do you remember the explosion when you were down with the warden? When you came up I said that the flat had rocked, but you said you thought nothing had come very near as the stuff seemed to be falling over the Park: well, honey, that particular bomb bust three houses at the end of the road!

'I have done nothing about packing up a suit case, as you suggested, and sending it out of London. Now that the bombing is less violent I really don't think it is necessary ... Gosh, that's funny! Three have just come screaming down, and by gawd we fairly rocked. Billy is under the sofa. Perhaps I'll do some packing after all ... There'll be another crash soon, the plane sounds angry. I'm heading for the Alcove and Girder. Sounds like a pub. So long!'

I went to my sister's flat at six o'clock. We were to eat there. We sat down and drank some sherry which, in the times I am speaking of, was still a drinkable thing and much enjoyed. My sister was not talking much, she was preoccupied. She kept looking at the clock. It said six-fifteen. 'I cannot understand it' she said. 'Have you the right time.' I said it was six-fifteen. This worried her.

We sat still. There was silence. The silence around us enfolded us like a shroud. We turned off the light, drew back the curtains from the window, and looked out. London stretched below us veiled and crouching, silent without sound, lying leashed and listening waiting underground.

A full moon swung in an indigo sky, drifting at ease along a line of fleecy clouds. Search lights flicked the horizon, restless and shifting, licking at the heavens with their darting tongues. They asked uneasy questions, but no answer came. They switched off suddenly, discouraged, snuffed. The silence extinguished them like a candle flame.

We returned to the fire. It was now six-thirty. My sister sat down, anxious, perplexed, lit a cigarette. 'I do not understand it' she said. 'They do not come as late as this. The signal should have gone by now. Something is wrong. I wonder what they are up to.' We waited. The whole of London waited. It seemed as though the night could not begin before its haunting overture.

It began without warning. The sirens wailed, in howling glissando, louder and louder the nearest one wailing, passing it on like vultures calling, rising and falling wailing and warning, summoning the men at arms to join the issue of this endless dreadful siege. The overture was over. Another raid was on.

We started to eat. In the distance we could hear it coming, the droning. Nearer it came, nearer and over, the slow throbbing drone of an enemy plane. Then another and another, another. In throbbing waves they droned their way, over and over enemy planes, German bombers flying through crests of fleecy clouds to blast their shells of fire and foam upon this cratered battered shore. 'They are making for Paddington' said Caroline, 'and Euston and Acton. We shall get it soon. Let's have some coffee.'

We heard the guns open up in the distance, then some muffled thuds. Our windows shuddered slightly. Another battery opened up, nearer, with short explosive pops. Then silence, thick, oppressive. Then a trembling silence, like the quivering breath that whispers in the coming mounting storm.

Another plane droned over nearer, nearer and overhead, and then passed on. We went on eating, but nothing tasted of anything. Feeding had ceased to be congruous.

Our minds were drawn inexorably upwards, upwards and over, over overhead, to that sinister droning as singly they came over, droning slowly over throbbing over head. We knew what happened when they pressed a button, when ever over anywhere they pressed it. We knew that anywhere they pressed it. We waited. The droning passed on slowly droning over, droning slowly over over head. We waited. Slowly droning over. Over, overhead.

'*Quick!*' cried Caroline. It happened in seconds. We leapt up Billy under sofa rushed corridor lay down. A thin scream sounded in the sky above and screaming with incredible velocity plunged screaming earthwards in a shrieking crash. A gun roared back defiance. The building shook. 'God' said Caroline, 'what a brute.'

We put the spoons back in their saucers. 'It has broken the ice' she said.

The barrage began. It hurled great chunks of sound around the place now near now far, now nearer, now next door. There was a mobile gun in the street below. The windows wildly rattled every time it barked. It made a wide strong open sound, filling the square with echoing rage like strident gongs struck hard with iron. We heard its shell bursts high in the sky, exploding like pods in swabs of cotton wool.

We turned the light off, stood by the window again. The moon still rode the fleecy clouds, immutably distant looking on untouched, immune indifferent, unearthed unwarmed unsung.

The moon shone pitiless upon these brittle little streets and homes, these spires these roofs and cornices, these palaces, these domes, these thoroughfares of teeming shops with jewels and furs and sparkling glass, and ivory, silver and gold and porcelain smooth and gentle to the touch as furniture moulded to our use; the fabrics of our mills and looms, brocades and satins chintzes velveteen, cottons and silks and patterned damask and linen cool and folded lovely as alabaster: these monuments, these statues to our past, these galleries these cinemas these pubs and bars and restaurants, this beating present where the shrill gay brilliance of Woolworths Lyons and Marks & Spencer bring to the multitudes the warmth and certainty of fusion, the gaiety choice display the tinsel and the symbol of a Christmas tree: this city this cosmopolis, this life this learning, this flesh this breath this breeding tissue of community, this land this earth this hearth this home with all the treasures of inheritance, this valiant struggling workshop of our puny selves lies open to heaven's indifferent gaze, cast and scorched in warfare's shame upon the altar of this heathen blitz.

Acknowledgements

I would like to thank the following for their help in the preparation of this volume: the staff of the Library of the University of Reading; Sandra Beynon; John Blackshaw of the Malvernian Society; Robin Darwall-Smith of Magdalen College, Oxford; Wendy Grisham and Alison Samuel of The Random House Group; Professor David Howell; Nigel Jenkins; The Reverend David Linaker; Dr. David Longbourne; Margaret Molloy of Christ Church, Oxford; Lorna Roberts of the Shropshire Records and Research Centre; Meic Stephens; M.F. Tighe; and Michael Webb.

Note on the Editor

N.H. Reeve teaches at the University of Wales, Swansea. His books include *Reading Late Lawrence* (2003), *Nearly Too Much: The Poetry of J.H. Prynne* (with Richard Kerridge, 1996) and *The Novels of Rex Warner* (1990).